PRAISE FOR *THE ANGRY TH....*

"When it comes to getting to the heart of the matter, John Kim's straight-to-the-point approach addresses issues that are often neglected with an honest, no nonsense attitude."
–Chris Spealler, CrossFit Park City/IconAthlete

"The best thing John does is to get me to honestly and truthfully assess myself and my situations by simple and uncomplicated statements. Then I'm able to take healthy actions built off those assessments! Thank you John!"
–Bill Grundler, Crossfit coach, athlete, commentator, gym owner

"Not only was John approachable and unique in his technique, he had a raw honesty that made me feel like we were in this journey together. My entire worldview shifted as a direct result of John's insight and encouragement. I needed his unique methods combined with my hard work in order to experience my rebirth. The result: I know my worth, what it feels like to actually love myself, and that gives me fearlessness in my personal and professional life. The kind of change and hope that John is actively engaged in bringing to people is the kind of radical change that most only talk about."
–Amy Chaffin

"John Kim is an amazing visionary! His methodology to life coaching is unique, refreshingly irreverent, and catalytic. His book is bound to be a masterpiece. It smashes conventional or outdated forms of psychotherapy. You can't help but connect to his work at the deepest level. This book will touch thousands more lives. Thank you John Kim!"
–ChaCha

"John frames complex ideas into powerful words that relate to us all. John lives the life, walks the talk and experiences the nectar he seeks. His words and energy inspire thousands of others to do the same. The community he has created and the lives he has directly and indirectly impacted are immeasurable."
–Beth Derrick

"I am a behavior therapist, and even though I enjoy my job a lot, I have always sensed a lack of accomplishment in my life. I work with autistic children, which is amazing, but something was missing. And then, through a friend, I discovered The Angry Therapist and his raw honesty made me want to be as honest in my life. I am a child again, playing around, jumping in puddles. It's not that The Angry Therapist has brought something new and exciting into my life, but John Kim helped me see how I could live in a way that, every day, I finally feel at peace with the little boy in me."
–Jean-Louis Ghazi

"You cannot ignore John Kim. He lets you know the real, raw details in the hope that you, too, will listen and see who you are, own it, say it, and use it for good. So you keep reading. You may laugh when he shares something personal, or you may cry. His story is compelling. But he's not stopping there. Be ready to look at your own shit. Now that you've been introduced to John Kim, you cannot ignore yourself."
–Julie Schilling

"I read John's book and it was a complete game changer for me. It was an incredible eye opener that I will never forget. Every other page was an a-ha moment. I'd never read a 'self help' book like it. His tools are refreshing, realistic, and most importantly, attainable. He comes to the table with a positive outlook that is inspiring, energetic, funny, and completely human. He has gifted me with the tools I need to repair my own cracked container, and has enabled me to build strong, healthy, mutually valuable, fulfilling relationships with others."
–April Policani

"As the Angry Therapist, John Kim manages to cut to the heart of the issues with a playful, no-BS angle. I have recommended his books and social media tribes to dozens of my yoga students. Within his work, I am held accountable to my own sense of purpose and happiness without feeling selfish or misrepresented. Many of Kim's simple quotes support me to not only celebrate my essence, but to inspire me to be the best version of myself while living my truth. And he cracks me up."
–Vanessa Running

The Angry Therapist

The Angry Therapist

A No BS Guide to Finding and Living Your Own Truth

John Kim

PARALLAX
PRESS

BERKELEY, CALIFORNIA

Parallax Press
P.O. Box 7355
Berkeley, CA
94707
parallax.org

Parallax Press is the publishing division of Unified Buddhist Church, Inc.

© 2017 Cover art by Josh Michels
Cover art and text design by Josh Michels
Author photo © Ja Tecson

Thank you to David Brooks and Marsha Shaw at Mission Grafica,
Mission Cultural Center for Latino Arts, San Francisco, California.

Printed on 100% post-consumer-waste recycled paper

Library of Congress Cataloging-in-Publication Data

Names: Kim, John (Psychologist) author.
Title: The angry therapist : a no bs guide to finding and living your own
   truth / John Kim.
Description: Berkeley, California : Parallax Press, 2017.
Identifiers: LCCN 2017004212 (print) | LCCN 2017012742 (ebook) | ISBN
   9781941529621 () | ISBN 9781941529614 (paperback)
Subjects: LCSH: Self-actualization (Psychology) | Self-esteem. |
   Interpersonal relations. | BISAC: SELF-HELP / Personal Growth /
   Self-Esteem. | PSYCHOLOGY / Interpersonal Relations.
Classification: LCC BF637.S4 (ebook) | LCC BF637.S4 K538 2017 (print) |
DDC
   158.1--dc23
LC record available at https://lccn.loc.gov/2017004212

2 3 4 5 / 20 19 18 17

CONTENTS

1   **Preface**

Introduction
7   **The JK Method**

Chapter One
11   **My Fucking Feelings**

Chapter Two
21   **The Power of Transparency**

Chapter Three
67   **Creating Your Stance**

Chapter Four
97   **Container**

Chapter Five
125 **Maintaining Your
Safe Container**

145 **Conclusion**

149 **Notes**

151 **About the Author**

This book is dedicated to anyone who has followed me on social media, read a post, watched a video, or liked a photo, and to anyone who has done a session with me—whether it was once or twenty times, via webcam, in a coffee shop, or around a lake. Without you, this book would not have been possible. You have given me more than likes. You have given me purpose, and for that I am forever grateful.

As far as we can discern, the sole purpose of human existence is to kindle a light in the darkness of mere being.
—CARL JUNG

Preface

The birth of this book was due to two events in my life. One: working as a therapist in residential treatment. Two: my blog.

For five years I treated teenagers struggling with substance abuse in a residential setting. I begrudgingly went to work every day in khakis and a dark blue Polo shirt (the standard uniform). I escorted kids on outings, went grocery shopping, and ran groups.

I felt more like a camp counselor than a therapist. It was not what I had in mind when I decided to go back to school at thirty-something to become a therapist. I'll tell you more about this part of my journey later. But through this experience, I learned about a treatment model called Therapeutic Community (TC). TC, intended for addiction treatment, originated in 1958, at a time when other systems of therapy (like psychiatry and general medicine) were not effective. The first TC for substance users was founded in California by Chuck Dederich, one of the earliest members of Alcoholics Anonymous. The basic idea of TC is that we can rebuild ourselves through others. We are not meant to go through things alone.

I was going through my own winter at the time—a divorce. We were young and pursuing the entertainment industry in Los Angeles. There was something romantic about two kids in love and dreaming big in tinsel town. But it burned faster than a Christmas tree. I didn't know what love was, and had low self-awareness. Her career was booming. I was frustrated. And the entertainment business isn't exactly a safe place to start a marriage. So it ended, or "expired" (a term I would use many years later when coaching clients through their break-ups.) I left with my SUV and a pillow. But it was a nice pillow, a Tempur-Pedic. She got the bed. I didn't know this at the time, but my divorce was the first domino that would start the process of my own rebirth. Through my own struggle, I came up with the concepts I would later use to help thousands. These concepts are what I will be sharing with you in this book.

I created a blog on Tumblr to express myself and share my journey. I made a choice to practice transparency, to pull the curtain back and show the world that therapists are real people too, have their own shit, and hurt just like everyone else. I quickly gained a following. People wanted advice. Then sessions. They seemed to connect to this Asian guy in a T-shirt and jeans, with bedhead and a love for motorcycles. My Tumblr became my Sangha, or Therapeutic Community.

My online practice spilled over into meeting clients at coffee shops, on hikes, and inside CrossFit boxes. I felt that if we were going to talk about life, why not do life while we were talking? This was a new image of how a therapist could look and practice. It gave me something I've never had before: a purpose.

WHAT MAKES THIS BOOK DIFFERENT FROM ANY OTHER SELF-HELP BOOK

This book is not an intervention—it is an invitation. I have also built you a safe container online, a virtual Therapeutic Community known as SHFT where you can rebuild yourself through others, no matter where you are in the world. It doesn't matter what you're going through; it's all about living a better life. This is my personal invitation to you to become part of a thriving community, so that you can always have the support you need in your pocket.

I hope to see you inside.

—Angry

Find your tribe at: www.shft.us
Meet me at: www.theangrytherapist.com

The JK Method

Self-help books are like bacon: they have a lot of fat. They're greasy, slippery, and easy to forget. The point of this book is to create one with less slip and more stick. Straight to the point. Less poetry, more practicality. My goal is to give you something you can actually use in your daily everyday life, instead of a collection of dense theories and concepts that will only collect dust on your nightstand.

I think we have made growth complicated. The commercialization of wellness has turned growth into a sales pitch. Growth has sold out. It's time to take it off the stage and bring it back into the garage. There's an easier way: I call it the JK Method. The JK stands for my name, John Kim, and it has less to do with my ego and more to do with the fact that I'm a C student. In order for me to digest and understand something, I have to break it down into its simplest form. My friends call it "John Kim-ing" it. Psychology is complicated. So for me to understand it in order to help others, I had to John Kim that shit. I've been doing it for the last decade. I came up with my own method for sustainable growth:

DIGESTIBLE + PRACTICAL = SUSTAINABLE

The key to growth is sustainability. Many embark on a journey to change, but it's short lived, like our New Year's resolutions. People approach change like a fad diet and yo-yo, getting some traction but then quickly snapping back to old patterns when they don't see the results they anticipated. Growth is not sustainable this way. Therefore, growth has to be worked into your daily life. It can't be something we do once in a while. It's something that should be a part of our daily living. I believe that if we design our life in a certain way, growth can be organic. When growth is organic, it is sustainable. This is the fundamental basis for my concept.

When people ask what I do for a living, I tell them I help build containers. What's a container? A container is your life space. This includes all of your relationships: with your partner, boss, friends, family, co-workers, and the relationship you have with yourself. If your container is cracked, your growth will be stunted. If your container is solid, your growth will flourish. I'll get into this more later, but cracks come from things like abusive relationships and dysfunctional families—our life experiences (situational or relational) that have caused us some version of trauma or pain. Cracks come from old blueprints we hold on to with both hands that don't allow us to follow our truth. Lopsided friendships that suck our energy, a painful breakup, an addiction, fighting an eating disorder—these can all cause cracks in your container. Building a new, safe container will allow you to maneuver more easily through life. It will protect you and allow growth to be natural and free flowing. My method is very simple. Build yourself a brand new container and growth will be organic. The process is broken down into three stages:

TRANSPARENCY
STANCE
CONTAINER

In Transparency, you are softening the soil that creates personal growth. This is preparation. It requires a conscious decision to be completely honest and raw with yourself. You will feel vulnerable and naked, but you must push through. The ground must be tilled. If you can't commit to this stage, you will not have the tools to move on to the next.

In Stance, you are planting seeds. You are driving your stake and envisioning your garden. This is the stage where you build the framework of your container. This framework will protect you and nourish the growth process.

In Container, you are baring fruit. You are reaping all the benefits of the hard work you put into building your container. You are maintaining your container by incorporating the concepts you've worked on into daily living, keeping the cycle going. Continuing to work all three stages will be the water and sun that keeps you growing and maneuvering at your highest potential. In the following chapters, we will explore these concepts in more detail. I will give you tools so that you can start living the life you deserve.

Chapter One

My Fucking Feelings

Therapists tend to be very private people. We do not disclose. It's not our fault. Textbooks drilled it into our heads in grad school. Our degrees slapped us with a very firm sense of should and should not. I am here to break confidentiality and turn labels on their heads.

I believe in transparency. I believe it is important that you know who I am in order for you to trust me with your story.

I believe in *with* you not *at* you. Many self-help books are distant, speak in third person, and don't give real life examples. I would like to bring you close, use "I" statements, and give examples from my own life. As you read this book, you will not only know how I work, you will also know who I am.

FLASHBACK

It's 9:17 a.m. on January 12, 2016. I'm sitting outside a small bakery, across the street from my new little apartment in Los Feliz, Los Angeles. They only have instant oatmeal. I hate instant oatmeal. It reminds me of who I used to be. Fast. Processed. Unhealthy. Nothing good happens that fast. I've learned that the only thing instant in life is our reactions, and I'm no longer interested in mine. Responses are where growth happens. Not reactions. Meaning and truth require patience and lots and lots of stirring. I want to be Mr. Steel Cut Oats.

I'm currently going through another expired relationship. It's weird how the universe forces me to stare at a blank page every time a relationship ends. It's like my treatment. In many ways, I feel like my life is repeating itself. I build something with someone. It ends. I take the lessons. Go through a mini-rebirth. Then build something with someone else. It ends. More revelations. Except I'm drinking decaf today. I've finally accepted that caffeine grips my throat too tightly, and I really need to breathe these days. Although things feel the same, a lot has changed since I wrote my very first "Fucking Feelings" nearly a decade ago. As I just typed that sentence, the last ten years flash like a trailer of a movie. For some reason, these moments stick out as pivotal ones in my story:

- Sitting alone in a rented room, freshly divorced, sipping coffee and writing blog posts on my new Tumblr blog, *The Angry Therapist.*

- Making silly YouTube videos, showing the world that therapists are actually human.

- Receiving my first ten bucks via Paypal for giving someone relationship advice via email.

- Hitting 20,000 followers on Tumblr.

- Running my first online group on my little white Macbook with people in different time zones, and thinking this is going to change everything.

- Finding a new way to get in shape called CrossFit.

- Getting my first tattoo.

- Buying my first motorcycle.

- Thinking about creating an online life coaching certification course and what that would look like—or if anyone would take it. The word "catalyst" hits me hard.

- Teleprompters, video courses, an article in *The Atlantic*, and two seconds on NPR. *The Angry Therapist* becomes an online ecosystem for people who need help, and life coaches who want to help.

- In a staff meeting with my start-up team downtown, creating a new app called SHFT that will connect all these dots and change the way we change.

- Sitting alone in a café sipping decaf coffee and writing my first published book.

Of course there are thousands of moments in between these: moments of stress, discouragement, all the *what-ifs,* and wondering if my journey has any meaning. There was a lot of trial and error, building things that didn't work, and feeling the weight of the giant boulder I was trying to push uphill. But today, I finally feel like the boulder has reached the top and is now starting to roll down the other side. I feel like it has its own momentum now. It's bigger than me. Some believe I've started a movement. By pulling the curtain back and showing people who I am and sharing my story, I've humanized the therapist. I've used the Internet as a therapeutic tool, and taught life coaches a different way into growth, one more simple and applicable. I've tried to connect people through tribes because I don't believe we're meant to do this alone.

I guess all of this changes the temperature of self-help—I'm not sure. I never set out to do anything. I just saw what worked and didn't work and followed my heart. I still see myself as the guy with a sweet tooth, self-doubt, and way too many dreams for this lifetime. I'm still trying to close the gap between who I am and who I want to be. I'm still inappropriate. I still write. I'm still learning about love. And I still talk about my feelings.

Or do I?

Well, that's the question I'm wrestling with these days. After I created a concept based on transparency, I started to wonder if I actually practice transparency. Just because I have a popular blog and help others process their feelings doesn't mean I am in touch with my own. Many have said that I'm different in person than on the page. That makes me feel like instant oatmeal.

Talking about my feelings is tough for me. I'm not wired to do so. I grew up in a family that only discussed numbers around the dinner table. There was no emotional cushion or modeling. I lived underneath a sense of panic created by my parents' fears of not living "The American Dream." They came here with two suitcases, five hundred dollars, and a desperate hope to give their two sons a real education. Mom worked fifteen-hour days in a convenience store where she was held up at gun-point many times, and dad pulled cable at a telephone company. My parents were always at work, so I was raised by pop culture. The only feelings I remember were from breakdancing, riding BMX bikes, and chasing girls. Those were the times I felt alive. It's odd that someone like me would grow up to become a therapist. I made a silly video once about "K-rage" (Korean rage). I defined it as a clinical disorder, stemming from the non-emotional space in Korean families. I guess I shouldn't say *all* Korean families— maybe just mine. But the universal laughs I got from the video told me there was some truth to it. When you don't have a safe space to express your emotions, you become angry. And this anger ripples into all areas of your life, keeping you stuck, frustrated, and grayed out. That was most of my twenties. Now I'm forty-two and I don't believe I'm angry anymore. I cured myself of K-rage. But I still struggle with tapping into my feelings and expressing myself. Besides the K-rage thing, I also think people who are good at listening to other people's feelings have difficulty listening to their own.

Maybe that's why I chose this profession—it may be a way to hide. But I'm not the only one wired this way: through my journey in coaching thousands all over the world, I've learned that most people have difficulty expressing their feelings. Most people grew up in families that didn't house a safe emotional space. Dad ruled with an iron fist. Mom distracted herself in front of a television. Siblings bullied us. Or mom was a supercareer woman who held all her emotions inside because she felt she needed to "hold it together." Or maybe our parents were picture-perfect. But our social environment or experience in relationships strapped a muzzle over our mouth. Whatever happened or didn't happen, no child enters adulthood unscarred. These scars fuck with our beliefs of what we're worth, what we deserve and don't deserve, and mute our voice and self-expression muscles.

So we grow up pulling from logic instead of our emotions. We become reactive rather than responsive. We suppress and ignore instead of address and release. This is how we survive. Instead of healing from our emotional scars, we cover them with Band-Aids made of "should have" and shame. We turn our emotional faucet off and start to concern ourselves with other people's feelings instead of our own. We lose ourselves. Over time, our self-expression muscles get weaker and weaker. Then, as adults, we can't understand why relationships are so difficult: why people say they feel disconnected to us; why we struggle with intimacy. Why we're not happy.

Our inability to express our state is what turns us gray. If we want to grow and live at our potential, we must start with how we feel.

EVERYTHING STARTS WITH HOW YOU FEEL. IT'S THE BIRTHPLACE OF CHANGE.

You're reading this book because you're interested in change. You're curious about new concepts and different ways into growth. In order to get there and practice them, you have to first start with this one question: Do you allow yourself to feel? In order to be, you must first feel. If you ignore your feelings or don't have the ability to express and validate them, your new path will have no direction. Although we may not all express our feelings, we all have the ability to feel. But many of us don't allow ourselves to. If not, why? Do you not want to go there? Are the feelings too painful? Do you feel like you don't deserve to have feelings? Do you think your feelings aren't valid or important? Or is it just habit?

Are you like me, a product of a nonfeeling based home? Why don't you allow yourself to feel? Or maybe you're on the other side of the spectrum? Maybe you let your feelings run your life. Maybe you can't control all the feelings that come up daily and it drains you. Either way, if you follow that string all the way down, you'll see that it's tied to your personal story. Somewhere down the line, you turned your faucet off and told yourself you don't need to feel anymore. Or you don't know how to turn it off and you've allowed feelings to force you into reactive states. One of your pistons is not pumping. Your engine is not running as it should. Whether you don't allow yourself to feel or you allow yourself to be overwhelmed by your feelings, this state is not accurate to your truth. You are not maneuvering at your potential. You are just living, not thriving.

As you're reading this, I want you to just be aware of where you fall on the spectrum. Don't worry about doing anything about it just yet. Know how you not allowing yourself to feel *or* allowing your emotions to get the best of you ripples through your life and relationships. The key word here is "allowing." At some point, you have given yourself permission. That means this is a choice. Just know that.

I may still struggle with expressing my feelings in relationships. I am still working on that. But I have no problem putting them down on paper. I've made a career out of it, starting with "My Fucking Feelings" ten years ago. I didn't put much thought into the post. I didn't say to myself this would be great marketing or a way to get followers. I didn't even know the value of followers at the time. There was no intention other than to just be me. I was struggling with the conformity of the therapist's journey. I felt like I was being run through a factory. That post was me ripping off my tie and tossing my DSM-V out the window. It was terrifying. I knew that my community would frown upon it, but there was no turning back. I was done pretending.

So I started posting "My Fucking Feelings" regularly, as well as pictures and videos of me CrossFitting, riding my motorcycle, smoking a cigar, everything I wasn't supposed to post as a professional but that made me human. As the fear faded, I started to feel alive. Blogging became my therapy. It made me feel alive. Allowing myself to feel and express my truth was the first domino in an empowering process of coming into my own.

The popular question in my line of work, "Who are you?" cannot be answered unless you have knocked down that first domino. Feelings are not just about feelings. They are about ownership. If you don't own your feelings/state, you will never know who you are. And if you don't know who you are, you will never know who you want to be. It's only when you listen to what you feel that you can begin to accept your story. Your story is the collection of events and milestones that has shaped you. It's the most valuable thing you own. Most people deny their story. They want to rip out chapters. But if that's how you spend your energy, you will never write a new one. You must start with your truth and eventually stand on it. And your truth is found in how you feel: about something, someone, your life, and yourself.

Giving yourself space to feel and allowing that to manifest into action is the process that will change your mindset. Experiencing something new, something real, something healthy, will give you fuel to continue down that path. Your behavior can change your thoughts just as your thoughts can change your behavior. It doesn't matter which hallway you enter. But to get there, the door you must enter is your truth/feelings. Instead of seeking something that is outside of self, like validation and approval, you must channel power from within. "My Fucking Feelings" opened my path, gave me a voice, changed my state, and eventually changed my life.

PRACTICE
My Fucking Feelings

Take a minute and play back your story. The good, the bad, the ugly. Everything. Take a deep breath, close your eyes, and see the unfolding of your life. What do you see? Don't cherry pick moments. Allow whatever to come up.

Trust that what comes up is coming up for a reason. Whether it's good or bad, it's meaningful to you. This means it's a part of you. Let your mind wander as you replay all the events that have led to where you are now. For now, do it in broad strokes. Later, we will do another exercise where we will go deeper with this.

What feelings are associated with what you're imagining? Don't think. Just see and allow yourself to feel. Chances are, there is pain. There is joy. There is regret. There is shame.

There is a collage of feelings that come up when you play your life back. Notice them. Don't judge them.

Another deep breath.

Now think about where you're at right now in your life and what you're going through. Feel your fears, worries, concerns, and struggles. What are you excited about, looking forward to, proud of? How have you changed, and how do you feel about that?

Take out a piece of paper. Or, if you're like me, open up your word processor of choice. Write across the top: "My Fucking Feelings."

Now write down everything you are feeling.

Chapter Two

The Power of Transparency

It all starts here. In order to build a safe container, you must practice transparency. Remember, a container is the mental, emotional, and physical life space around you that will protect you and promote your growth. You must rebuild your container to make it safe. And the first step to this is practicing transparency. Without transparency, there is no soil. So let's define what Transparency means.

Transparency means not only being honest with others but, more importantly, with yourself. Taking a real hard look at where you're at in your life, including the way you think, what you internalize, your unhealthy behavior patterns, and how your actions affect others. Transparency also means practicing self-awareness.

> Look at the evidence and be willing to question your own truths, and be willing to scrutinize things that you hold dearly because that way, that transparency, that self-awareness, will protect you from ever becoming somebody whose beliefs somehow make them have myopic vision about what could be.[1]
> —Jason Silva

The highest currency you'll ever have is self-awareness. Without it, it's impossible to know what you need to change. Usually, people achieve awareness by getting chopped at the knees over and over until they realize something needs to change. Or they never have the realization, and life just becomes one giant endless ocean of suffering. If they accept that, growth becomes a very small island, quickly fading away. But you haven't accepted that because you're reading this, which means something or many things have happened for you to at least be curious about yourself, and wonder if changing yourself can lead to a better life. You may have a general sense of what you want to change. The universe may have told you in some form or another: perhaps through your relationships, life events, how people respond to you, how you react to them. Transparency means fully accepting all of it, taking full responsibility for where you are. No more blaming. No more playing victim. You are here. This is your truth.

Transparency means accepting your story. Most people want to rip out chapters and forget what happened. Of course, because most of us have been through a lot of shitty things, we had no control over a lot of things. But your story is unique, and believe it or not, it's the most valuable thing you will ever have. It's what makes you different from any other person on this planet. Since I hate numbers, let me give you a visual interpretation of the chances involved in you being born who you are, and everything it took to form your exact DNA. Say you set a turtle into a random ocean somewhere in the world. Then you tossed a life jacket into another random ocean in the world. The chance of you being born is about the chance of that little turtle popping his head through the hole of the life jacket—on the first try.

If you spend most of your life trying to deny your story, you'll never reach your potential. Here's why: Your potential is activated when you are giving—and by giving, I don't mean feeding the homeless. I mean being in a state of sharing your unique gifts. To get there, you have to be maneuvering into a state of authentic or honest self. If you are consumed by and/or holding onto all of the shit that has happened to you in the past, it blocks that process. You are now taking. You are sucking energy: being angry, resentful, and discouraged. This cycle leads only to giant tubs of ice cream, a television, and a sunken couch.

> There are times in my life when I have been medicine for some while poison for others. I used to think I was a victim of my story until I realized the truth; that I am the creator of my story. I choose what type of person I will be and what type of impact I will leave on others. I will never choose the destructive path of self and outward victimization again.[2]
> —Steve Maraboli

It's a process, but if you want to practice Transparency, you have to make the choice to start accepting your story. As this happens, the past will have less power over you. Eventually, you'll get to a tipping point where your past will start to empower you. But you will only reach that point when you start giving yourself new experiences, and start to have different beliefs about yourself.

WHEN I WAS A SCREENWRITER

Here's an example: I used to be a screenwriter before becoming a therapist. A part of me wants to rip that chapter out of my life because I feel like I failed at it. But the truth is, if it wasn't for that struggle, I would never have become a therapist. It was the conversation I had with my own therapist about my pains and frustrations with the screenwriting business that encouraged me to go back to school—which I would not have ever done on my own in a million years—and study psychology. And because of that, I started a blog, built a practice, and so forth.

Our story unfolds because of the choices we make and the events that occur in our lives. We have to believe in this progression, in this trajectory of connecting dots. You have to accept everything you went through in order for you to be who you are and where you are today. Even if you are not satisfied with who you are and where you are—which most of us aren't—acceptance is required for change to happen. Acceptance gives you the first step to step up on. Without it, there will be no traction moving forward.

So what does it look like to accept? It's different for everyone. For me, there are two parts. First, it means to make peace with the past. That's not just a choice; it's a daily practice. You have to make up with your past as if your past was a person you got into a horrible fight with. Apologize, say what you need to say, explain, forgive, whatever it takes. Make the past your friend—although you don't have to be best friends. But you can't want your past to die.

The second piece to acceptance is refusing to live anywhere but the here and now. By accepting the past, you are making a choice to no longer live in it. The tipping point is when you not only accept your past but also appreciate all of the things that "went wrong," whether they were situational or relational, and know that they were pockets of learning. Without them, there would be no opportunity for growth. The difference between accepting and not accepting your past is the difference between feeling owned and empowered. If you feel that life owns you, maybe it's not about bills, shitty relationships, or lack of purpose—maybe you haven't fully accepted your story.

> Owning our story can be hard but not nearly as difficult as spending our lives running from it. Embracing our vulnerabilities is risky but not nearly as dangerous as giving up on love and belonging and joy—the experiences that make us the most vulnerable. Only when we are brave enough to explore the darkness will we discover the infinite power of our light.[3]
> —Dr. Brené Brown

TRANSPARENCY = VULNERABILITY

Transparency also means being vulnerable. There is tremendous power in vulnerability. Author Brene Brown has spent a lifetime doing research on this. Says Brown: "Vulnerability is the birthplace of innovation, creativity, and change." Vulnerability requires emotional exposure, but it doesn't mean that we verbally vomit on people. Being vulnerable involves responsibility. Let me "John Kim it" by saying that vulnerability is having the courage to show your true self even when you feel unsafe. Vulnerability is about always pulling from your heart: with friends, at work, everywhere. And men, this doesn't mean that you're being weak. There's tremendous strength in showing yourself. Being weak is walking with a veneer and choosing to be someone you're not. Most people do this out of fear. We're afraid of what people might think about us. Transparency means shattering that veneer.

> When I am afraid to speak is when I speak.
> That is when it is most important.
> –Nayyirah Waheed

Practicing Transparency is like a muscle. The more you exercise it, the stronger it will get. It's not a one-time thing. You must thread it into your daily life, like your diet and your fitness. That's the only way you'll see results.

LIFE AS A MOVIE TRAILER

It was the first group I was asked to run at my new job as a therapist in a private treatment center for eating disorders. I wasn't supposed to run groups until the next week. I was "in training," which meant enjoying a chicken curry sandwich and a cappuccino in my office as I soaked in how cushy this job was compared to working in non-profit. Suddenly, the head therapist popped his head in and said *we're short*. He wasn't referring to our height. I had to think of an intervention, quick. Although I'd literally run hundreds of groups, I felt like this was my first time. I began doubting my own skills. This fear made me break into the treatment center's interventions file. These exercises were proven to work. It was my way of being safe. I found one called "The Human Knot." I thought it was appropriate since the group was titled *Experiential*.

Before we executed The Human Knot, I came up with a quick exercise off the top of my head. This would be the appetizer before the main course. Since it was more of an appetizer, I didn't feel like it needed to be a real intervention. But what was really happening was that by taking the pressure off to be a good therapist, which meant using what other therapists use, I allowed my true self to speak. By not looking at the exercise as a "real intervention," I was able to relieve the pressure on myself and stretch my creative space. It allowed me to relax in a way that would position myself to hit flow.

In positive psychology, flow, also known as "the zone," is the mental state of operation in which a person performing an activity is fully immersed in a feeling of energized focus, full involvement, and enjoyment in the process of the activity. This increases performance in whatever you're doing. In essence, flow is characterized by complete absorption in what one does. Flow happens when outcomes are removed and we focus strictly on the here and now. Athletes, artists, musicians, and writers all tap into their flow states. It's when they are the most creative and at their peak performance. It's when time disappears.

> It is when we act freely, for the sake of the action itself rather than for ulterior motives, that we learn to become more than what we were.
> —Mihaly Csikszentmihalyi

It's almost impossible to hit a flow state when you are pulling from a false version of you. My authentic self had his own ideas, and during that group I allowed him to speak. Here's what he said:

> *Take a minute and imagine all the important events that have happened in your life up to this point. Now, string those scenes together any way you wish and picture your life as a movie trailer. Describe the trailer as if you just saw it and you're telling*

a best friend about it. Tell us what's happening from a visual standpoint, what you literally saw. If there's music, voice over, or dialogue, describe that as well.

Those were the exact instructions I gave my clients as I got out of my head and allowed my truth to take the wheel. I knew this was my truth speaking because it was very John Kim. I love movies. I am a very visual person. I am unrehearsed. The intervention had me written all over it. You'll know your truth because it's organic, not forced. You can feel it: It feels like you. Your truth leaves room for improvisations and things to unfold in ways you did not expect. That's where magic happens. When we're operating from anything but our truth, we are cut off from the possibility of sharing our greatest gifts, our own uniqueness. Pulling from our truth, or our Solid Self, which I'll get into later, creates the x-factor that can't be duplicated.

Using visual imagery to stir up emotions was extremely effective. One girl described a scene where she tried to commit suicide by hanging herself but fell off the chair. It was a dark comedy. She laughed. Another girl saw a scene within which she was bleeding and couldn't go on. She cried. Another described her most intimate day with her husband. Hers was a romance. The intervention sparked the group to take on a life of its own. They were swimming. It did what it was supposed to do: ignite emotion and create dialogue. For the next hour, we processed what came up and how they felt about it. The members then supported and encouraged each other. They felt less alone, less damaged. They had revelations about themselves and what they wanted to change. Growth was happening.

After the movie trailer exercise, I decided to execute The Human Knot as planned. They did the exercise, but seemed to just go through the motions. A few admitted that they had done it before. Of course they had: it was in the sharing file. At the end of group, I asked which exercise they enjoyed more. Everyone couldn't stop talking about the movie trailer and how much came up for them. The movie trailer exercise was me being transparent. The Human Knot was me trying to be my perception of a "good" therapist.

I did not share this story to brag about the effectiveness of my interventions. The point of this story is to show the difference between operating from a true version of yourself and a false version. The false version is a widget. It is made in a factory created by society, friends, family, and old blueprints. It spends a lot of time going back and forth from the past to the future. The true version of yourself is unique, one of a kind and lives in the here and now.

Do you want to be a widget or a work of art?

Whether you're at a party, on a date, grocery shopping, or thinking about which intervention you want to use at work, fight your false self. That's where we live the most false moments of our lives.

> We are all lies waiting for the day when we will break free from our cocoon and become the beautiful truth we waited for.
> –Shannon L. Alder

TRANSPARENCY = CONTRIBUTION

IF YOU DIED TOMORROW

I spent my twenties in the corners of dark coffee shops, desperately beating my brain for snappy dialogue and seamless act breaks—all to sell the million-dollar screenplay. It was my ticket into the quad, where cheerleaders and football players talk about parties and prom, the address of "The American Dream." If at that time someone asked me, *If you died tomorrow, would you feel okay with your contributions on earth?* I would have said *no* without any hesitation. I was a starving writer. My life hadn't even begun yet. It was on hold. I was on hold until I had a house in the hills, a three-picture deal, and my own office on a studio lot. Although I had sold a couple of scripts, I had made no real contribution to this world, only words on a shelf and a desperate desire to chase a rainbow made of Coca-Cola.

Recently, I asked myself the same question: *If I died tomorrow, would I feel okay with my contribution on earth?* I saw faces of all the kids and families I've been treating: their tears, their smiles, and their laughter. Then I saw all of the people in my personal life: the authentic friendships I've made with them and their unconditional love for someone with nothing to offer but a worn heart and a dull ear. I saw the people I've been helping on my blog, through emails, questions, and webcam sessions. I've heard amazing stories, hopes, dreams, and revelations. I saw my team of Catalysts who help me run my coaching courses and champion my message. And finally, my team at SHFT who are helping me take the "I" out of self-help.

I don't have a mansion, sexy cars, or a beach house in Malibu. I'm just a guy who practiced transparency and has ideas about changing the way we change. But it's the first time in my life that I feel like I've actually made some kind of contribution in this world. So yes, today I would feel okay if I died tomorrow. Not that I want to die. And it doesn't mean I'm done. Actually, it means the complete opposite. It means I've finally let go of chasing shiny things, things that aren't real.

WHEN YOU STOP CHASING, IT'S NOT THE END. IT'S JUST THE BEGINNING.

It took a family business, marriage, and my own personal growth to finally have the courage and tools to redefine for myself what is valuable, meaningful, and worth fighting for. It required being okay with myself and my defects and knowing what I have to offer. I couldn't have done this without being transparent, creating a Stance, and building my own safe container.

Many times we have to go through our own personal death to start living again. People don't usually change until they are forced to. Usually something is at stake: a marriage, children, sobriety, property, meaningful relationships, or our health. But death sanctifies life, and the truth is that we can die tomorrow. We can die walking across the street. We can die driving to the supermarket. Our lives are so monotonous and safe that we forget this. We choose to live in a bubble that makes us feel like we're going to live forever. We wrap ourselves with our fear blanket that doesn't allow us to stretch our life muscles. We think this will protect us, but the truth is that it keeps us confined. Popping that bubble and leaning into daily discomfort is where you will find life. We must pop our bubble often, because comfort sets in fast. Popping our bubble doesn't have to mean a complete life rebirth. It doesn't have to mean leaving marriages, changing careers, making a new batch of friends, or moving to the other side of the world. Popping our bubble can consist of small everyday things, like making an effort to change our unhealthy thinking and behavior patterns. These all contribute to breaking out of our cocoon so that we can share our gifts and head down a path toward a limitless life. Every day is another chance to leave something behind—to move, teach, support, encourage, entertain, help, raise, invent, define, create, and change.

> It doesn't matter what you do, he said, so long as you change something from the way it was before you touched it into something that's like you after you take your hands away. The difference between the man who just cuts lawns and a real gardener is in the touching, he said. The lawn-cutter might just as well not have been there at all; the gardener will be there a lifetime.[4]
> —Ray Bradbury

PRACTICE

If You Died Tomorrow

Ask yourself, *If you died tomorrow, are you okay with your contributions?* Is your work done here on earth? Do you have anything else to give? If so, what? Yes, what you have to give can change. It probably will. But what is it right now today? And most importantly, what is stopping you from making your dent?

PSEUDO VERSUS SOLID SELF

Murray Bowen, an American psychiatrist, was among the pioneers of family therapy and founders of systemic therapy. Beginning in the 1950s, he developed a systems theory of the family. His large contribution was the idea of differentiation from other people. Bowen describes a differentiated self as a Solid Self, and a fused self as a Pseudo Self. The Solid Self knows what it needs and desires, while the Pseudo Self reacts to those around it. The Solid Self is non-negotiable with others and is composed of an individual's firmest convictions and most integral beliefs. Pseudo Self consists of others' opinions absorbed as one's own without any conscious commitment to the beliefs underlying the opinions absorbed. As a person becomes more differentiated, the importance of hard-core self increases and the influence of Pseudo Self correspondingly decreases. In an unhealthy relationship, two Pseudo Selves come together and fuse into each other, one person losing and the other person gaining self. This is when you lose yourself in another person. It happens often. It might have happened to you. You meet someone, fall in love, or in lust. You spend every minute together, because you think that's what loving someone looks like. You start thinking like him or her, like things that they like, compromising or ignoring your own likes and wants. Gradually your life starts to revolve around the relationship/your partner. Then one day, you wake up and don't know who you are anymore. You've lost yourself. You've traded your awareness of self for the comfort you find in your partner. Your container is cracked.

The Solid Self, however, maintains its individuality and does not merge. The Solid Self has beliefs, opinions, convictions, and life principles. The Pseudo Self is a product of emotional pressure. The Solid is not. The picture society has painted of romantic love is pseudo based. The idea of "the one" and everlasting love can distort our lenses into believing something is healthy when it's not. The powerful feeling dysfunction and co-dependence produces can be mistaken for "soul mates." Some of the most powerful relationships we've been in have also likely been the unhealthiest. Healthy love is two Solid Selves coming together.

The path to the Solid Self begins with Transparency. People with weak transparency muscles live within a Pseudo Self.

This is a false version of you. It seeks other people's approval and validation. You live in Pseudo Self because it gives you a sense of security. It allows you to hide and live in disguise. But most importantly, the Pseudo Self straps a muzzle on your gifts. By gifts, I don't necessarily mean talents. I mean what makes you different from any other person on the planet.

In screenwriting, they say what's most important is your voice. Everyone has a story to tell, but it's your voice that makes your script stand out from the rest. For example, Quentin Tarantino has a very strong voice. It comes out in his dialogue and his non-linear way of storytelling. Being your Solid Self gives you a voice.

> A writer should have this little voice inside of you saying,
> tell the truth. Reveal a few secrets here.
> —Quentin Tarantino

A good way to remember Pseudo versus Solid is false versus true. Pseudo is false. Solid is true. Everyone has a true and false version of themselves. Many times, where we pull from depends on our environment and who we're around. For example, if we're surrounded by people we want to impress, we tend to project an idea of what we believe they are looking for or attracted to. Our dial is turned on Take instead of Give. We are seeking something from them: attention, validation, approval. In order to turn that dial back to Give, we must pull from our truth. We must be transparent in voice and self. This adds solidity. What we are giving is our true self. Everything false clouds the picture of our true self. Transparency cuts through the clouds. What most people don't understand is that being transparent and pulling from our truth is not just a choice. It's a practice. Growth is not a diet. It is a lifestyle. This means we must live it daily.

It's difficult to listen to our truth. We're not used to doing it. We're afraid of rejection and what others may think. But the thing is, we're all afraid. If we weren't, we wouldn't be human. We're afraid of failure, rejection, public speaking, death—the list goes on and on. And we can work on those fears and probably will for the rest of our lives. But if we are afraid of ourselves— afraid to *be* ourselves—we create a prison. And in this prison, we are not able to share our unique gifts. We are not giving. We are taking. And since life is about giving, we are not living. You must shatter the fear of being your true self or you'll snap back every time you stretch. Of course, this is a process. It takes time. But you must make a decision to start the process, and hold onto it knowing what's at stake: your potential. As a friend, brother, sister, husband, wife, teacher, mother, daughter, father, son, leader, visionary—everything you do. Everything you are. But everything you are isn't about you. That's how you break through your fears. Your truth isn't about you. It's about the world experiencing your potential. Your truth is greater than you.

The other part of this is ability and habit. Many of us have spent our lives putting others before us. This knee-jerk reaction has prevented our ability to even know what our truth is. Without this ability, we disappear. We become grayed out like an app that's stuck updating. We must learn to discover our truth. Finding our truth is uncomfortable. It means we have to listen to ourselves. We talk to ourselves a lot but rarely do we listen. So what does listening to our truth look like? It means to not only be aware of our truth but stand on it. There is action involved. Play out what is honest to you. The more you do it, the easier it gets. And if fear creeps in, remember it's not about you. It's greater. Many people around you will resist your truth because they're not used to that version of you. You'll be changing the dynamic of all your relationships. Some may even expire because of this. This is what people call outgrowing others. But you have to hold on and push through, or you'll always be living someone else's life and not yours. And the world will not experience the true you. The people who fall off are preventing your growth, so let them go. And the people who accept you and your truth are valuable since they will be sharpening you.

The Pseudo versus the Solid Self was a primary theme in the movie Fight Club. If you haven't seen Fight Club, I'll tell you about it. (Spoiler alert.) The film is ultimately about inner conflict. We find out at the end that Edward Norton's character and Brad Pitt's character are the same person. Who do you think is the Pseudo Self and who do you think is the Solid Self? When I ask my class this, most people say the Edward Norton character is Solid and Brad Pitt is Pseudo. They say this because they think Brad Pitt is the "bad" guy or antagonist. But the truth is that Brad is the Solid Self and Edward is the Pseudo Self. Edward Norton is lonely and lost. He hates his job. He can't sleep. He feels disconnected with the world. He's just going through the motions of life like a walking zombie. Then he meets Brad Pitt. Brad challenges him, his fears, and his thinking. Edward begins to change through their interaction. He finds his voice and becomes a leader. Edward Norton goes from Pseudo Self to Solid Self. Or, simply put, he goes from false to true. Without truth, nothing can be built.

> Only the truth of who you are, if realized, will set you free.
> —Eckhart Tolle

THE POWER OF A SANDWICH

I once bought someone a sandwich. I was getting a quick dinner at a local deli when I noticed an older gentleman sitting by himself. He was just sitting there, bobbing his head to the music. He didn't look homeless. He just looked lonely. We made eye contact and he nodded. I quickly turned back to my book, shoved the rest of my sandwich into my mouth, and thought to myself, *Maybe I should buy him something to eat.* That thought was my Solid Self— my instinct, my gut, my truth speaking. He had a soft tone. I could barely hear him. Then my Pseudo Self kicked in, a loud thundering voice that convinced me that the man didn't need a sandwich. Pseudo came at me like a lawyer—logical and cold. *What if he's just waiting for someone? He would be insulted if I asked him if I could buy him food. Maybe he's the owner?*

But these were just excuses to stay in my comfort zone. I finished my sandwich and was about to leave when I stopped myself and thought, *Wait a minute. This isn't about him. This is about me. If I leave, I am allowing the part of me that was formed by abuse, failed relationships, dysfunctional family dynamics—all the shit that's happened to me in life that's lowered my self-worth and security—to control me.* All that, just because I wouldn't buy someone a sandwich?

It's not about the sandwich.

It's about allowing your voice to be heard, giving yourself permission to be the true version of you before life slapped on a veneer. If I leave, I add glue to the beautiful fake porcelain smile. If I turn back and go with my initial gut, I may crack that veneer. My dial turned, as did I. I bought the man a sandwich. My Solid

Self was happy when the man smiled and nodded at me. The man allowed his own Solid Self a voice when he smiled at me, a stranger. My Solid Self didn't want this to be weird. He wanted to acknowledge connection.

By buying a stranger a sandwich, I allowed my Solid Self to be heard. I drove my stake into the ground and told my Pseudo Self to fuck off. Fuck off for every time he made me critical of myself, doubted my worth, and allowed others to define me. I left the deli feeling a little more powerful than when I arrived, and it had nothing to do with their flatbread. Many of you reading this may think I'm crazy for trying to squeeze so much meaning out of such a simple act. You may be telling yourself, *Man, this guy's really reaching.* Make a note of that voice. Recognize it. That is your Pseudo Self.

PRACTICE
Pseudo Versus Solid Self

Think about your life, from the time you wake up to the time your head hits your pillow. As you replay your typical day, ask yourself, *When am I my most Pseudo Self and when am I my most Solid Self?* Really think about it. When you're with your family, at work, with friends, at the gym. Think about all the different communities you engage with throughout the day and week. Where do you feel you are your most true self and why? Most likely, it's where you feel the most safe. Where do you feel you are the most false version of yourself and why?

Write down all the areas where you feel the most pseudo. For each, write down one thing you can do to start feeling more solid.

STOP LIVING YOUR LIES
Your beliefs will determine where you will go. They are like rudders in your life journey. Many people have heard this before and

agree with it. But they take no action to change their beliefs and so their lives don't change. If you want to change your life, you *have to* change your beliefs, starting with your beliefs about self.

Take two people. Person one believes she doesn't have much to bring to the table in relationships. She doesn't believe she has any value. Person two believes she has a lot to bring to the table. She believes she has tremendous value. The behavior and energy of person one will be very different than person two. Agreed? In her dating experience, person one will be in a seeking state, pulling from Pseudo Self as she seeks validation and approval, and will most likely compromise. This will make her less attractive and the chances of her being happy and fulfilled in a relationship are low. Due to person two's beliefs about herself, she will be maneuvering more in her Solid Self. This will create space for her unique gifts to shine, making her more attractive as well as attracting the same, increasing her chances of being happy and fulfilled in a relationship. One's belief in self manifests into behavior and shapes one's life.

> Beliefs have the power to create and the power to destroy. Human beings have the awesome ability to take any experience of their lives and create meaning that disempowers them or one that can literally save their lives.
> —Tony Robbins

Unless you come from a perfect family and have had nothing but flawless relationships, which is impossible, you have false beliefs about yourself. We all do. And behind those beliefs is a broken record playing songs of judgment and criticism. Of course, the volume of the record varies, depending on your story. But we all have this playing inside us. It is quicksand. We must break these records. So how do we start to dissolve our false beliefs so our behavior and energy can change?

You must stop living your lies.

The first step is to find out what your lies or false beliefs are. You will do this exercise on paper later. But for now, think about the beliefs you carry with you that you know are not true. You only believe them because you feel that way. But feelings are not facts. You've heard this and know this. Just because you feel a certain way doesn't mean you are that feeling. Second step. Put on your detective hat and search for proof. Why do you believe this? Did someone tell you something? Did something happen that caused you to choose this belief about yourself? At some point in your life, you made a choice to believe this. When was it? What caused it? Now put a bookmark there and let's talk about your emotions.

Sometimes our thoughts and beliefs stem from our emotions. Hopelessness, loneliness, despair, sadness, and anxiety. We attach how we feel to who we are or what we can do. We sink deeper as our raw emotion turns into an emotion-driven thought. This is how we get negative self-talk loops stuck in our heads. You say something enough and you will start to believe it. Whenever the Pseudo Self drives the mind into patterns of thought that are contrary to the Solid Self, these thoughts can turn into trouble. The tracks of our broken records turn into false beliefs. They start to define who we are and limit our potential. *The world would be better off without me. I'd be better off drinking again. No one loves me. I am worthless. I don't deserve any better than this anyway. I can't. I can't. I can't.* These false beliefs create fear and uncertainty. They keep us locked in our heads on a planet very far from joy and happiness.

Accept your feelings, but not the judgmental thoughts behind them. Allow yourself to feel whatever feeling that is truthful, then let it go—it is temporary. You must separate your feelings from your identity and worth. This is an ability that takes practice. Every time you feel a negative feeling, know that it's just a feeling, like a cloud passing. It's not attached to you. Accept your feelings, sit with them, then allow them to pass. The last piece is the most important. Most people hold on to them with both hands until they start to internalize those feelings.

Feelings don't define your worth, unless you allow them to. And so many do without even knowing it. It's okay to feel lonely. It's not okay to stamp yourself as unlovable. It's okay to feel discouraged, overwhelmed, frustrated, and confused. But it's not okay to believe you are inadequate or can't accomplish something because you currently feel like you can't. It's okay to feel hurt because someone decided they didn't want to be with you. It's not okay to believe you are defective.

THERE'S A DIFFERENCE BETWEEN HOW WE FEEL AND WHO WE ARE.

So how do we separate the two? How do we live in our truth instead of our heads? How do we detach our feelings from our worth and abilities?

ACKNOWLEDGE

The first step is to acknowledge how you feel. Feelings don't disappear because you ignore them. They will only grow louder. Many believe if you ignore your feelings, they will go away on their own. The truth is that they will build up. If you want to release, you must first own. The more you try to ignore or suppress your feelings, the longer they will stay inside you. This is how resentment builds. This is when we use shame to emotionally cut ourselves. Be aware of how you feel. And don't judge your feelings. They're just feelings. Just because the feelings feel bad doesn't mean you are bad. Know that. Scan your body. Notice how your feelings manifest physically. Allow them in. Then sit with them for a bit. It's like squeezing your muscles to release tension. The more you acknowledge and fully accept how you feel, the easier it will be to release them.

EXPLORE

After you have allowed yourself to feel your feelings, the next step is to explore where those feelings are coming from. It's important that you allow yourself to feel first, so that you feel heard. If you jump to exploring where your feelings are coming from without allowing yourself to feel them first, there is room to minimize your truth. You are not letting yourself be heard. Fully accept and feel first. And let that take as long as it takes. But not to the point where you are drowning in them and letting them control your life.

Many times our feelings are triggered from events that have happened in the past.

Explore that with gentle curiosity. This is the learning piece, the beginning of the growth process. The goal is to see if there's a pattern to those feelings and what the triggers are. Again, you're not judging or arguing with your feelings. You're exploring where they are coming from. Maybe someone has hurt you in the past and what happened recently has triggered that experience, so what you feel is amplified. Maybe you're feeling fear because what you're going through now feels familiar to something you went through before. Maybe someone cheated on you and the person you're dating now is acting in a way that reminds you of that. Or maybe it's deeper. Maybe your dad left early on and when you feel someone being distant, you feel the rejection again. Once you learn why you feel the way you do *when* you feel the way you do, you can start to trace things and connect dots. You can start to pull back and understand yourself and your wiring better. You can make it about you instead of about other people. This understanding is what leads to change. Without this understanding, it's easy to get lost in your feelings and let them lead you. Since we often hold on to and dwell on our negative feelings rather than the positive ones, we will often be lead by our negativity. This is when we can become highly reactive and make decisions we will later regret.

FIND YOUR WHY

Figuring out the *why* is where you'll find traction. Our motivation comes in our *why*, not our *what*.

Why do you react?

Why do you feel anger when he says that or behaves that way?

Why does that hurt you so much?

Why do you always go to *that* place?

Why do you run?

Why do you hide?

Why are you attracted to that type of person?

Why do you put so much pressure on yourself?

Why do you do see the things you do?

Why do you always see it that way?

Why do you fall into that thought pattern?

Once you have a better understanding of your whys, you can make healthier choices about how to respond to your feelings and triggers instead of reacting to them. Remember, this is a process. It takes time. Be gentle and patient with yourself.

REVELATIONS
The next step is to gain awareness through your revelations (or what many people call "A-ha moments.") You realize you think a certain way or discover a pattern that you keep falling into that prevents your growth. Going back to your feelings, what are some of the conclusions you make about yourself or others because of the way you feel? Again, feelings are not facts. Once you discover the whys, you may realize that just because you feel something doesn't mean your conclusions are true. Be aware of the messages you tell yourself. Put yourself in an observer position and notice them. What does that say about you, how you think and behave? What revelations do you have about yourself by going through this process?

EXECUTION
The final step is execution. Take all this information you've learned about yourself—how you think, how events from your past effect you today—and apply the changes to your daily life. That's execution. How are you going to take your revelations (what you learned about yourself and your thinking) and apply the new changes into your everyday life? What does that look like in action? For example, one revelation may be that when someone doesn't text you back within ten minutes, you panic and think they're going to leave you or that something is wrong. You've

realized that this feeling stems from your fear of abandonment. Your mom left you at an early age. Now that you know this, you can talk yourself off the ledge when he or she doesn't text you back within ten minutes. You can put on your detective hat and conclude that there is no evidence that feelings have changed or that anything's wrong. The more you prove your old self wrong, the more you will shed your old beliefs and create new ones. Execution means you're breaking a pattern. That's where growth lives.

GROWTH IS FIFTY PERCENT REVELATIONS AND FIFTY PERCENT EXECUTION. WITHOUT THE EXECUTION PIECE, ALL YOU'LL HAVE ARE IDEAS. NOT CHANGE.

Remember this. I will mention it many times. So many people who want to change their lives spend their time consuming information and sparking revelations, but they don't push what they've learned about themselves into their everyday lives. That's where the real work is.

How do your thoughts and conclusions play out in your life? What is the behavior attached to those thoughts? Does that behavior match up with who you want to be?

Go back to false beliefs and lies. Apply the same steps. I kept it brief so you can just read it for now. We'll do it on paper shortly.

Acknowledge: Acknowledge that you have beliefs that are false. Acknowledge that you are living lies and pulling from these lies is directly affecting your life potential.

Explore: Where do your false beliefs and the lies that you are living stem from? Dig deep.

Find Your Whys: Why do you have these beliefs? Did something happen? Did you tell yourself something that changed what you believed about yourself?

Revelations: What did you learn about yourself through this process? How do your false beliefs play out in your life? What thought and behavior patterns do you need to break?

Execution: From your revelations, what changes do you need to apply to your everyday life? How are you going to start doing this? And more importantly, when?

PRACTICE
Stop Living Your Lies

Let's start with a visualization exercise.

Imagine for a moment that you didn't have the false beliefs that you do. Imagine if you didn't live with your lies. How would your thinking and behavior be different? How would that impact your life? Sit with it for a minute. See it. Play it out. Visualize what your life would look like.

Now write down what you see.
Is this life different than the one you're living now? If so, how?

Okay, now let's go through the steps on paper. Don't rush this process. Take your time with it. Maybe do one step per day. Make sure you put a lot of thought into each step and be thorough.

Acknowledge: Acknowledge that you have beliefs that are false. Acknowledge that you are living lies and pulling from these lies is directly affecting your life potential. Think about this. You don't have to write anything down.

Explore: Where do your false beliefs and lies stem from? Dig deep. Think about the first time in your life when you had that belief. If you can't remember, think about the first time your action or behavior matched that belief. What sparked that behavior? Write it down.

Find Your Whys: Why do you have these beliefs? Did something happen? Did you tell yourself something that changed what you believed about yourself? Write it down.

Revelations: What did you learn about yourself through this process? How do your false beliefs play out in your life? What thought and behavior patterns do you need to break? Write it down.

Execution: From your revelations, what changes do you need to apply to your everyday life? How are you going to start doing this? And more importantly, when? Write it down.

THOUGHT PATTERNS
Now let's talk about your thought patterns.

Write down five problematic thought patterns that reoccur in your life. What are the common ways of thinking that you keep falling into? For example, I'm always thinking about the future or dwelling on the past. This prevents me from living in the present, which affects my relationships as well as my state and energy.

A lot of common problematic thought patterns fall under cognitive distortions. Some common cognitive distortions include black and white thinking, overgeneralizing, jumping to conclusions, etc. You can Google them. But I don't want to limit you with only the distortions you find on the Internet. Before you research cognitive distortions, think about your own thought patterns. The more specific they are, the better. Play out your thought patterns and write down how each translates into beliefs and behavior. Then write how each belief and behavior affects your life and how you feel about yourself. Give examples. Be specific. Finally, write down what new behavior or thought can replace the old ones. When are you going to start implementing these new thoughts and behaviors?

You have just created a map of change for yourself.

All you have to do is follow this map and there will be a shift in your life.

CUT YOURSELF IN HALF

As an exercise, I asked a group of women I was treating for eating disorders to imagine their future selves, the person they want to be, the version of themselves they were striving for. Then I asked them to write a letter from that future person to who they are now, offering advice, wisdom, and encouragement. After they did the assignment, we processed it in group. I asked them what the experience was like. Many of them said they noticed it was much easier to give themselves compliments and encouragement as their future self rather than their present self. I asked them *why*. They said it was because writing a letter from a future version of themselves allowed them to separate themselves from a false self, and to step out of their minds for a minute. They were able to leave their false beliefs and negative thoughts about themselves behind. I asked them if they would be able to verbalize what they wrote in the letter to themselves in the present time, right now, if they were alone in front of a mirror. They all said *no way*.

By shifting their lens and living outside of self, they were able to accept compliments and encouragement more than if they were inside their minds. In group, my clients were able to love themselves more by living outside of self. I wondered: If they were able to be encouraging and gentle with themselves in a letter, could they start being that way off of the paper? Most of them had low self-esteem. They were extremely hard on themselves and their behavior that had lead them to their disease. The letter proved that they had the ability. Now it was a matter of practice. They needed to cut themselves in half. Let go of the old—all of their false beliefs, broken records, thought patterns—and start pulling from the new, the best version of themselves. The cut is what's important. It means there is a before and an after. It sets your mind up to lean into something new, and release the old.

PRACTICE
Cut Yourself in Half

Imagine the highest self-actualized version of yourself. Imagine how that person thinks, behaves, and what she believes about herself. What's her energy like? How does she enter a room? How do people respond to her? What are her gifts and what does she have the ability to do? Now write a letter from that person to you. What would the future version of you tell yourself today? Maybe all the lessons you've learned and how to maneuver through life better? Maybe you need to remind yourself who you are and all the gifts you possess? But the goal isn't to force praise. Be real with yourself and write something honest. That's more important.

Now that you've written something from a different perspective, you have a better understanding and feeling of what your future self is like. Imagine embodying that future version of you. Like a spirit taking over a body, your future self is now inside you. Notice the new energy. What does that feel like? All the things you imagined your future self to be is now inside you: how your future self thinks, feels, and acts. The old has died. The new breathes inside you and speaks a brand new language.

> For it is not what happens to us that determines our character, our experience, our karma, and our destiny—but how we relate to what happens.
> —Lama Surya Das

There is the old. And there is the new. When you find yourself getting in your head, pulling from false beliefs, and playing old records, know that that is the residue of your old self. Pull from your new, future self by allowing that person to speak. Listen to this new you and do what it says and feels. Daily, moment by moment. Feel the future version of you, the one that wrote that letter, living and breathing inside you. It will be scary and awkward at first to allow that version of you to be in the driver's seat. But the more you allow and trust your future self to guide and dictate your choices, the higher your potential will be. Your potential doesn't live in the old you. It lives in the person you always imagined you would be. But you don't have to imagine anymore. It's already inside you. You just have to listen to her and allow her to live.

PROVE NOTHING

Now let's add another layer to maneuvering in your solid state. Most of us go through life always trying to prove something. We want to prove that we're right, that our opinions matter, that we're not stupid, that we can love in a healthy way, that we are successful, and so on. It all comes back to our worth. We try to prove to others (but especially to ourselves) that we have value. We want to believe we're worth something. And proving it once isn't enough. We need constant validation. But when we are in a trying-to-prove-something state, we are pseudo. We are seeking. We are wanting. In this state, we block our unique gifts, lowering our potential.

Say you're at a party and you find yourself acting a certain way to fit in. That's your false self (Pseudo Self). You don't want to be your true self (Solid Self), because that may mean you'll stick out or run the risk of people not liking you. Being in a Solid State and practicing Transparency means you are just being you, in your truest form, at every moment. This is extremely difficult. Think about it. Throughout the day, when are you purely just you? Most likely that only happens when you are alone. I think many of us live different versions of ourselves depending on where we're at and who we're around. The less you seek approval, the more transparent you are. The thing is, you're not the only one in the crowd displaying your Pseudo Self. Others are also. So when you show your Solid Self, people notice. Some will not like it, but some will. You will start to attract people who see you for you. These people are valuable. They will be part of building your new container.

In my early thirties, I turned my family's restaurant into a scenic supper club in Hollywood. It was a heavy lunch but slow dinner business near the studios. We did everything we could to get the night business up, from live music to sushi—although was an Italian restaurant (that's the Korean way of doing business, sell whatever you can). But nothing worked until I met a promoter. He was an actor trying to make money on the side. I was unsure of him but we had nothing to lose.

Our little family business slowly morphed into a nightclub. Within two months, the club blew up. It was written up in the trades and suddenly became a hot spot with a strict guest list: only models and millionaires. I remember sitting at a table with Fred Durst from Limp Bizkit, a movie mogul, and a billionaire who owned a sports team, and thinking: What the hell am I doing at this table? I remember getting a call from Kate Hudson, asking Leonardo DiCaprio where he wanted to sit, and hanging out with Matt Damon in the VIP trailer after hours. I had a lot of friends then. People were nice to me and gave me a lot of attention. There was cash everywhere. And yet when I look back, all I feel about those days is how small I felt because I wasn't my true self. I was operating in a pseudo version of myself to seek approval and validation. My friends weren't friends. They were people who didn't want to wait in line.

Today the only thing I have to offer is me. No comped meals, no entrance into a shiny make-believe world, no exposure, no connections. Just me. Love it or leave it.

I have nothing to prove.

WHEN YOU HAVE NOTHING TO PROVE, YOU HAVE THE MOST TO GIVE.

I no longer feel small. The people who are in my life today value me as a person, not because of what I can do for them. I admit I do have fewer friends now then when I ran the club. That said, when I was living from my Pseudo Self I wasn't authentic, so how many of those were actually true friends? It's not that I have less friends today—I just have more real ones.

d to being in an environment where you're
true self, it will feel weird at first to suddenly
esidual feelings of wanting to give something
it's what I was used to, even though it wasn't
taking. It was difficult to just be myself and
believe that that was enough. I felt naked, raw, and vulnerable. I
had nothing to hide behind.

So my work was about leaning into the uncomfortable place
where I allowed myself to just be real—to be me—without feeling like I had to give people things to validate my worth. Like
breaking any pattern, there is often a tug that draws you back
to who you used to be and how you used to think. But the more
I maneuvered into my Solid State—the more I proved nothing
to anyone—the more I started to cultivate a new relationship to
myself. That's the key, because that's when you start to rewire
yourself. I've discovered that it's nearly impossible to have a new
relationship with yourself when you're constantly trying to prove
things to other people. When you make the choice to prove nothing, the true you shows up. Connecting to and embracing this
true you is where your potency lives.

TWO KINDS OF TIME

We live in three different time spaces: the past, the future, and the
present. We shuffle back and forth throughout our day, but we
mostly live in the past and the future. What happened yesterday?
What's going to happen tomorrow? What will happen to me in
five years? What's for dinner tonight? How am I going to pay my
bills? What if I never find "the one"? And on it goes.

Okay, so let's simplify this. There are actually two kinds of
time: healthy time and unhealthy time. Healthy time is living in
the now. Unhealthy time is living anywhere else. What does living
in the present have to do with being transparent? Transparency is
a state that centers around your truth. If you are constantly living
in the past or future, you are not living your truth. You are living
in what was, which can be distorted, or the unknown, which is
not real. Transparency means to be here, the only honest space.

Most of us spend our days dwelling on the past or obsessing
about the future. We get up in the morning thinking about all
the things we need to get done in the day. On the drive to work,

we analyze past relationships, our accomplishments, our failures, those expensive shoes we're waiting to go on sale, the potential raise, our credit card bill, the date last night, the party this weekend. Then at work there are more to-dos, rehearsing presentations in our heads, wondering why we're gaining weight, losing our hair, why he didn't call, she didn't write, reminding ourselves to stop being a pushover, debating what we want for lunch, how to change our parents, talk to our boss, address our lover—and suddenly the day is over. Now we're in bed, replaying the day and where we could have done more. We have trouble going to sleep, which means we wake up grouchy as we start our mental machine all over again.

This becomes a pattern that waters us down into zombies who drag through life clenching lottery tickets and a grudge. If we want to change the future, we must focus on the now. That's where our power is. Everything else is an illusion.

> As soon as you honor the present moment, all unhappiness and struggle dissolve, and life begins to flow with joy and ease. When you act out the present-moment awareness, whatever you do becomes imbued with a sense of quality, care, and love—even the most simple action.[5]
> —Eckhart Tolle

YESTERDAY

First, let's talk about the past. This includes everything that has happened up until this very moment: five minutes ago or five years ago, it doesn't matter. Whatever's stored in your memory, it's okay to remember. Not living in the past doesn't mean that we forget about the past. A lot has happened that may have left imprints in your heart and brain. No one enters adulthood unscarred or without trauma. Shit has happened that you had no control over; unexpected events transpired that were unfair to you, and these events made you angry, afraid, regretful, and wired you a certain way. This wiring created unhealthy thought and behavior patterns that affect you today. They are the foundation on which you built your Pseudo Self.

Your Pseudo Self won't allow you to accept your story, often because you believe your story *should* be written a certain way, instead of allowing your story to unfold from your truth. Your Pseudo Self reminds you of everything you did "wrong" in the past and shames you for it. It tells you that you must be better because you're not good enough. It wants you to internalize this unhealthy thinking and judge and devalue yourself. If you let go of the wheel, your car will always swerve into pseudo, because you have a past like everyone else—and your past is powerful. Living in it will keep you away from your Solid Self.

So how do we let go of all this—everything that's happened to us that feeds our Pseudo Self? Well, let's start with the words "to us." We use passive words a lot when describing the past. This happened *to me*. That happened *to me*. The problem with "to me" is that it puts us in victim mode, and when we believe we are or were victims, we become powerless: We go into a state of hiding and self-protection. We are instant prisoners. "To me" is the lowest state to be in.

You must stop playing victim. Change your language. Things didn't happen *to* you—they happened *through* you. What happened is all part of your story and you must accept it. The more meaning you find in all the events that have lead to where you are now—and the more you own them—the less you will feel like a victim.

IF YOU BELIEVE YOU WERE A VICTIM, THE PAST WILL ALWAYS HOLD YOU HOSTAGE.

Your true self has already accepted your story. It encourages you to live in the present.

TOMORROW

The future and the unknown are scary. I've struggled with this my entire life. I don't know about you, but I want an amazing life—one with meaning and purpose and financial security. And not knowing if that's ever going to happen is terrifying. Yes, I can tell you that I do feel purpose and meaning these days, but I can also tell you that I want two homes, a Korean barbeque in my backyard, and a collection of motorcycles. If I didn't, I'd be lying.

I could also tell you that we have the power to create our own destiny and that we can make anything happen, but that would just be me being my Pseudo Self, because that's what I believe life coaches are supposed to say and what you want to hear. The truth is we can't really *make* anything happen. That's a conceit of the positivity feel-good movement and it's bullshit. Tragedies happen: people die of cancer, addiction, get hit by cars, shot at—well, you know. You live on earth. We aren't superhuman. We have to learn to stay empowered and at peace with ourselves and with the world at large (and not become a victim) even when shit happens—because it does and will.

But we can live a certain way that facilitates good stuff to happen—where we attract good things, healthy people. Yes, there will still be tragic events and shitty days, but we won't be crushed by them. Instead, we will see them differently. They will become opportunities for learning and growth that make us wiser and stronger. So it's not about making things happen. It's about being in a state where we get out of our own way and allow our gifts to shine. That's when we get unstuck. That's when good shit happens and we can grab happy. The beginning of this process is living in healthy time.

> The power for creating a better future is contained in the present moment: You create a good future by creating a good present.
> —Eckhart Tolle

TODAY

One way to stay in healthy time—and swipe your past-dwelling future-tripping state clean—is to practice gratitude. Before you roll your eyes, let me tell you my story with gratitude. I always thought that gratitude was a wellness buzzword until I started to practice it. That's what separates the eye rollers (and I used to be one of them) from the believers. What does it mean to practice gratitude? Practicing gratitude doesn't mean that you're grateful only when good things happen. That's easy and noneffective. By that definition, most of us practice gratitude at least three times a year: Thanksgiving, Christmas, and our birthdays. But let's look at that. Really. Take those three days when most of us are honestly grateful: What does that day feel like? How stressed are you on Christmas? And I'm not talking about the stress of the holiday; I'm talking about when things have settled and you're sipping eggnog and opening presents with your family. How angry are you when you're saying everything you're thankful for during Thanksgiving? How sad are you on your birthday when your friends take you out to dinner, sing to you, and give you presents? What if we can channel those positive feelings daily? You can.

> Gratitude unlocks the fullness of life. It turns what we have into enough, and more. It turns denial into acceptance, chaos to order, confusion to clarity. It can turn a meal into a feast, a house into a home, a stranger into a friend.[6]
> —Melody Beattie

Here's the thing about gratitude: If you don't practice it daily, it will be nothing more than a trending wellness buzzword, like I mentioned above. In the world we live in today, it's extremely difficult to want less, because we naturally want more. And there's nothing wrong with that, as long as wanting more doesn't keep us obsessing about the future and focusing on everything we don't have.

We rarely practice gratitude daily. Unfortunately, it's often when we have a real health threat that we snap into shape and experience deep, profound and life-changing gratitude—the kind that keeps us living in the fullness of the moment. Most of us need that type of wake-up call to change our mindset. But often our gratitude moments are fleeting, and we quickly snap back like a rubber band into our sticky thinking. In order for gratitude to actually work and stretch the experience—to clear your mind of anxiety and promote peace—you must practice gratitude daily and consider that we have enough: that there is good in our relationships and that we can build something with what we already have. This is what clears our mental and emotional canvas and gives us space to paint again; this is what keeps us in healthy time.

> Acknowledging the good that you already have in your life is the
> foundation for all abundance.
> —Eckhart Tolle

Remember, living in healthy time doesn't mean never reflecting on events from the past or thinking about the future. It just means not dwelling or obsessing, and not allowing yesterday and tomorrow to define today. Today is where our power lives.

The final tip about how to live in healthy time is to anchor, which means to use all your senses during an activity to bring you into the here and now. We are almost always in our heads. We rarely focus on and appreciate what we see, hear, smell, taste, and feel. These are all powerful tools that help bring us into the moment. When I'm feeling stressed, I grab my helmet and go on a motorcycle ride. It's one of the sure ways to clear my mind. When I'm on my bike I have to be completely present or my life is at stake. Yes, I may drift for a second or two, but if my wheels are spinning, I'm completely aware of everything around me. I'm aware of the wind, sounds, smells, the feeling of the clutch, shifter, and throttle. Everything is heightened. And the result is that I am completely present and out of my head. I am anchored in the experience, in the moment.

I also anchor myself in fitness: I do CrossFit. I use all my senses when I'm working out. I see the digital red numbers counting down on the clock. I smell the air and sweat. I feel the movements in my body. I hear the community and loud music. I take everything in and it snaps me into the present. And when I'm fully present, I'm tapped into a flow state where time disappears and I'm performing at my best. It doesn't matter what the activity is. You can anchor anything: eating, sex, writing, driving, dancing, going to sleep. The more you anchor throughout the day, the more you will train your brain to live in healthy time.

Like everything else, anchoring is a practice. It's done daily.

Here are my anchors on a typical day:

Wake up. I'm not really a morning person. Not much anchoring here. I just try to get out of the house as fast as I can to start my day. The longer I stay in bed, the harder it is for me to get up. But once I leave my house, my turbo kicks in. For some reason I hate being at home. I think because my home doesn't really feel like home right now. Of course, this is less about cool furniture and more about my mindset. That's something I need to work on. Be that as it may, my senses don't even kick in until I'm in my car.

Drive to work. I roll the windows down and turn up the radio when I drive. I anchor myself by taking in the outside air, the music on the radio, and the scenery. Even though that scenery is mostly traffic and people, I try to see things that I wouldn't usually notice. Today, for example, I noticed a man on a pink bicycle wearing bright red earmuffs and pajamas. I thought, *Wow, there's someone pulling from his Solid Self.* When I anchor, driving becomes an experience instead of another part of the day to be overwhelmed with thoughts.

Answering emails. Not much anchoring here. This is just plowing ahead, face in the dirt. And I'm okay with that.

Vlogging. When I do my video blogs, I anchor myself by forcing myself to take a breath, then I just hit record without any rehearsal. This forces me to be fully present. The result is a fresher vlog, and less burnout for me. If I spent a lot of time outlining and rehearsing to make the "perfect" video, the pressure of that would strip me of my essential experience. It would take the fun out of the process and keep me in my head.

Writing. I need to use all of my senses to write. I need coffee or a hot beverage. I need a visual space like a coffee shop. I need people's energy. I've tried writing without all these elements and I just can't do it.

Lunch. This is a great opportunity to anchor and practice mindful eating, but I admit that I rarely anchor when I'm in front of food. Like so many people, I inhale my food instead of using all my senses to truly enjoy and appreciate my meals. I usually leave with a stomachache. This is something I need to work on.

Fitness. Anchoring is key for me during my workouts. If I don't focus on using all my senses to be fully present, I just end up going through the motions instead of enjoying the process. You may argue, *Well who really enjoys working out?* Try anchoring and see if it becomes a different experience. Can you imagine doing yoga without being present? Instead of it being a mind-body-spiritual experience, it would just be stretching.

Dinner. I know I mentioned I struggle with anchoring when I'm in front of food, but if I'm eating out, anchoring comes naturally for me. I really enjoy eating out by myself. I love sitting at the counter in diners because there's so much culture there. I love taking in the people, the music, and the atmosphere. Eating becomes an entirely different experience. No stomachache.

Making love/having sex. Okay, I'm going to go there. This is one of the best activities to anchor because you're sharing the experience with another person. Yes, you can share other experiences, like enjoying meals and working out, but you don't share those experiences on the same intimate level. We've all had flat boring sex and mind-blowing sex. The key difference is not love—it's presence.

Going to bed. This can go in one of two ways: I can lie in bed and allow my mind to drift, which means I start thinking about everything. Living in unhealthy time like that will surely set me up for a poor night's sleep. Or if I make an effort to anchor myself—to meditate and focus on my breathing—I'll have a good night's sleep.

> Feelings come and go like clouds in a windy sky.
> Conscious breathing is my anchor.
> —Thich Nhat Hahn

PRACTICE
Two Kinds of Time

I could tell you to write down five things you truly feel grateful for before you go to bed every night, hoping that becomes a powerful routine that keeps you in the here-and-now instead of the past and future. But if you're like me, you'll do it once or twice and then get lazy, or go through the motions until it quickly fades. So instead, I would rather you experience something.

Feel your state right now as you read this? What's on your mind or been on your mind that is causing anxiety? Is it tied to something in the past? Are you comparing past events or relationships to current ones? Is there anxiety about something that hasn't happened yet? Are you worried about what's about to come or that something might not happen? Feel it, without judgment.

Take a deep breath.

Now focus on what you are grateful for today, right now. What do you have in your life that you truly feel grateful for? Your partner? Kids? Friends? Your health? A stable job? Your new car? What about how far you've come?

Think about five things you are currently grateful for right now. As you think about each one, really soak in it. Why are you grateful for those things? It doesn't matter how big or small they are as long as they are honest. Take your time with this. Sit with it. Make it a spiritual experience. This is important. It allows it to be greater than you.

Before your mind drifts into worry and pulls you back into unhealthy time, how do you feel? If you truly feel gratitude, then you will notice a shift in your feeling. There should be a sense of calm, even if it's mild and temporary. You should feel more present and purposeful—and hopefully you'll want more of that experience. It's there for you and it's free.

Everyone has their own way of practicing gratitude. Some enjoy writing about it. Some prefer to focus on it during meditation. Some like to actually acknowledge their gratitude by telling others how they feel. It doesn't matter how you do it. What matters is that you practice it daily.

Here are some tips:
Commit. Like any discipline, you have to first make a decision to do it. Don't "try it." Commit to it. Say you'll do it diligently for a month without it being contingent on results. Without a commitment, the experience will be short-lived. Gratitude gains momentum over time and with practice, so start strong by committing to a certain period of time. Just begin. Thinking about it and coming up with a solid plan doesn't matter if you never begin. Don't procrastinate. The longer you wait, the more it will drop down on your to-do list.

Gratitude is not a mental exercise. The power lives in the feeling of it. Allow it to start at your heart and percolate through every cell in your body. Embody it. Embrace it. Let it live inside you. Make it a spiritual experience. Practicing gratitude will make your world bigger.

Eventually, gratitude will become a mindset, not just a daily exercise. This will not only help with your practice, but it will change you as a person. It will make you less reactive and angry, and more filled with love and purpose. Share this experience with others. Gratitude can be extremely contagious. The more you spread it, the more it will grow inside you.

> When you realize there's nothing lacking,
> the whole world belongs to you.
> –Lao Tzu

Anchor a daily activity that you usually don't anchor. It can be eating, driving, or making love to your partner. The goal is to experience the difference, because experiences are convincing.

RETURN YOUR BOWLING SHOES
Every Sunday morning, I sit down with my friend (spiritual

mentor, brother) at a local breakfast joint in Silver Lake to sip coffee, process life, and inhale chocolate croissants. One morning, he gave me some great advice about the anxiety I had been experiencing in a new job. What he said hit me hard because it was so simple: He said *don't own it.* I thought about this. Then I thought about it again. He was absolutely right. If I don't own it, it won't own me. The fight you had with your boyfriend, the date that went south, the transition of a new job—these events are not yours to own. They were a gift from God, the Universe, whatever higher power you believe in. They are yours to borrow and learn from.

We create anxiety when we clutch onto things and try to control them. We do this with our children, our relationships, our jobs, and ourselves. But if you believe you do not own the event/ experience, it won't have power over you. This doesn't mean that you shouldn't own your feelings. Your feelings are valid and you should own them, because they are your truth. But the shit that's happening in your life is separate from you. You are borrowing those experiences like a pair of bowling shoes: you get to use them as tools. Without ownership, there is no urge to control.

GET RID OF THE DESIRE TO CONTROL AND THE BURDEN IS SUDDENLY LIFTED.

What if you saw the event or relationship that is bringing you so much anxiety as a teacher? How would that change your mindset? For example, parenting a teenager, with all their angst and difficult behavior, can be extremely taxing. Teenagers don't like to be controlled. But as a parent, if you can't control your teenager, you might feel extremely out of control yourself. You might experience tons of anxiety and conflict with both yourself and your teenager.

But what if you saw your experience with your teenager as a "teacher"? What if you understood that there is learning to be found in your exchange, no matter how challenging? Would that allow you to let go of the tug of war rope? Would that make it easier for you to be in a neutral but open place and let go of things that you previously would have tried to control? If so, how would that mindset affect the relationship with you and your teenager? In a positive way or a negative way? And would the change in the relationship create less tension and more peace?

Simply choosing to see an event or a relationship as a "teacher" can create the space that allows you to not own things. If you're not a parent, what if you saw your friend as a "teacher"? Your boyfriend? Your co-worker? Or better yet, the person you have the most friction with—someone you dislike and can't stand. What if you saw them as a teacher in your life? What lessons are they teaching you?

In the practice of tolerance, one's enemy is the best teacher.
—The 14th Dalai Lama

DON'T OWN THE BULLSHIT

Another thing we tend to do is to own other people's stuff. We all bring into adulthood unresolved issues from our childhood that we've internalized. Maybe they were mean or cruel things someone said or did, or a burning criticism that was more about the person doling out the bullshit than it was about us. Whatever it was, we often internalize these things for so long that we eventually forget where they originally came from. Instead, we engage with the bullshit: We believe it, we own it, and eventually it undermines our sense of authentic self.

When you don't own other people's opinions, feelings, behavior, and past, you also don't have to own the anxiety that comes with it.

There's an old parable about not owning or accepting another person's anger that goes something like this: Buddha used to walk into a city market every day and pass a bitter, verbally-abusive guy who would hurl insults at him. Every time the Buddha passed him, he'd simply smile and walk on. This went on for weeks. Finally, one day, the old bitter guy asked Buddha why he endured his insults without reacting. And the Buddha famously replied: "If someone gives you a gift and you do not receive it, to whom does the gift belong?"

Okay, so we're all not like the Buddha, but you get the idea: You can choose to accept the gift and own the bullshit, or you can decline it. When you decline it, you give the bullshit back to the person doling it out. It remains their bullshit, not yours. You don't internalize it, believe it, or own it.

TRANSPARENCY MEANS NOT OWNING WHAT'S NOT YOURS.

PRACTICE

Set Your Bowling Shoes on Fire

Make a list of everything you tend to own that is not yours. Go as far back as you wish. If it comes up, you're owning it in some way, which means it's probably owning you. Here are a few things I own today that I need to return:

- Other people's inability to cope with their own bullshit.
- Other people's opinions and perceptions of me.
- Other people's expectations of me.
- Other people's definitions about what's right, what's wrong, and how life should be lived.
- Other people's stories.

Come up with your own list.
Then burn it.

SHARE YOUR STORY

Sharing your story doesn't mean verbally vomiting on someone. It means being vulnerable and disclosing when appropriate. You have to define what *appropriate* means for you. For me, if the desire to share is driven by my ego or coming from an attention-seeking place, then it's probably not appropriate. If that desire is rooted in using my story to help someone or to form an authentic connection, then it is appropriate. Sharing your story is a gift, and giving is being transparent.

Say that you were at a party and learned that someone was going through a divorce. She admitted it to the group of single people you were chatting with. The discussion was about how difficult it is to find *good honest friends in this town.* Since her divorce, she has not been able to find new friends. It was courageous of her to disclose this, since society tends to stamp *defective* on your forehead when you are divorced.

Now say that you were also going through a divorce. If you decide to share your story, you are giving. You are giving someone support and making them feel less alone. Of course, you could have alternative motives, but only you will know what your true intentions are. There is power in sharing stories when they are coming from a giving place. We learn more from other people's stories than we do from our own. If no one shared their stories, where would we be? What lessons would we learn? How alone would we feel?

Sharing your story isn't just about helping others and forming connections; it's about allowing yourself to be heard. It's crucial for you to allow yourself to be heard, because when you are heard, you are accepting your story and owning every chapter. Most people want to rip out certain chapters from their story because they're lined with shame. But there is no self-acceptance if you don't own your entire story. And self-acceptance is what growth is built on. Without it, there is no healing. Sharing your story allows you to heal and access your true self rather than deny it.

We are all a million walking stories. Your story is what makes you *you.* Your Pseudo Self will want you to close your book. Your Solid Self will want you to open it. Transparency means to accept, embrace, and share your story.

PRACTICE
Share Your Story

Write your story. Or if you feel brave, say it on video. Just use your phone; no need for any fancy editing—the less polished, the better. Start anywhere. Make it as long or as short as you'd like. Tell it backwards; it doesn't matter—do what feels comfortable. Now post it on my *The Angry Therapist* Facebook page. I can feel your panic from here. That page is full of stories, mine as well as others. But someone, somewhere will read it and it will affect them. You will be giving, and the process will be empowering. You will also allow yourself to be heard and will practice accepting your story.

> Stories are the shortest distance between us and truth. So when we understand and uncover these stories, we gain the opportunity to understand maybe we need a new story.
> —Chris Cade

THE MAGIC MOMENT

INT. THERAPY OFFICE- DAY (2003-ish)

JOHN KIM sits in front of his THERAPIST, a silver haired man in his fifties, sporting a wrinkle free shirt and a bright tie.

>   THERAPIST
> How was this week?

>   JOHN
> Instead of talking about that, can we talk about my career?

THERAPIST
Sure.

JOHN
I don't know if I want to pursue it anymore.

THERAPIST
Why not?

JOHN
Sitting in coffee shops all day writing dialogue and trying to
come up with the next big idea isn't as exciting as it once was.
I'm sick of being a starving artist. It's affecting my marriage.
Also, I feel like I'm getting older.

THERAPIST
You are not a starving artist. You've sold scripts.
You're a working screenwriter.

JOHN
I never wanted to be a writer. It was a way to direct.

THERAPIST
Why do you want to make movies, John?

JOHN
I want to move people. It's why I loved Legos as a kid. I want
to create something and watch the expression on their faces when
I show them what I made. I want to make them feel something.

THERAPIST
If you couldn't make movies, what would you do?

JOHN
I've wanted to make movies since I was ten.

THERAPIST
If you couldn't.

John thinks about this long and hard. He looks down,
staring at his therapist's bright candy colored socks,
then looks up and says under his breath—

> JOHN
> I want to do what you're doing.

Silence. The therapist looks confused,
as if he didn't hear correctly.

> THERAPIST
> What?

> JOHN
> If I can't do it for the masses, I'll do it one at a time.
> If I can't make movies, I want to be a therapist.

The therapist thinks about this.

> THERAPIST
> Then do it.

> JOHN
> I'm a C student. I hate school.
> There's no way I'm going back. No. Fucking. Way.

Soon after this therapy session, I found myself in a classroom.
I was back in school, this time studying psychology instead of
film. I found my voice and fought my Pseudo Self. I stopped
seeking approval and following my old blueprints of what success
looked like, and started living outside of self (my head). I began
to embrace and share my story, not owning what wasn't mine. I
exercised Transparency.

IN A SHOT GLASS
To be transparent:

- Fight your Pseudo Self (live your truth).

- Stop living your lies/false beliefs.

- Live in healthy time (in the here and now).

- Don't own it (let go).

Accept, embrace, and share your story (give instead of take).

Chapter Three

Creating Your Stance

Now that we've softened the soil, it's time to plant seeds. In Transparency, you are allowing yourself to be you. In Stance, you are not allowing anyone to take your true core away. This isn't just about having boundaries—it's more than just digging a moat around your castle. Stance means driving your stake in the ground that supports your Solid Self. Your Stance will define your character.

In CrossFit, your core determines everything. All movements stem from it. It's where you find energy and balance—through Kettle bells, rowing, thrusters, wall balls, sit-ups, pull-ups, push-ups and all of the Olympic Lifting movements. Without a strong core, you become a leaf. There is no power. It's impossible to be good at CrossFit without a strong Stance. Your center is the center of everything.

This is true for all sports: surfing, skating, wrestling, football, baseball, martial arts, yoga, dance… on and on. It's the same for life. Your Stance will give you a solid core and determine whether you live grayed-out or at your potential. It will either protect you or destroy you, and ultimately determine who you are.

YOUR STANCE: THE FRAMEWORK MADE OF NON-NEGOTIABLES THAT HOUSES YOUR TRUE SELF.

When I was in my twenties, there wasn't much I wasn't willing to negotiate. The type of car I drove was dependent on whether my best friend approved of it. What I wore, my hairstyle, and the act breaks in my screenplays were determined by my girlfriend's taste and opinions at the time. I did things that I didn't believe in, like pouring well vodka into premium vodka bottles at my family restaurant's bar to make my parents' lives easier. I was moldable and had no spine. The people around me influenced my choices and determined who I was as a person.

After my divorce, I realized that I didn't have any non-negotiables. What are non-negotiables? First, I want to make the distinction between a non-negotiable and a preference. Say you will only date men who are six feet tall with baby blue eyes and a six-figure income. Those aren't non-negotiables; those are preferences (and narrow ones, in my opinion). Non-negotiables are not just things you prefer. Rather, they are iron-clad standards that determine who you want to be.

NON-NEGOTIABLES: THINGS THAT YOU ARE NO LONGER WILLING TO NEGOTIATE ABOUT YOURSELF BECAUSE THAT SHIT DIDN'T WORK.

Having non-negotiables means drawing new lines with a Sharpie, not with chalk. By drawing those lines, you are telling yourself you have worth. Even if you are unsure of your value, having non-negotiables will protect you from events or people who strip you of your sense of value. In theory, no one can take away your value but yourself. In practice, however, we allow others to take away our value all the time. Having non-negotiables circumvents this possibility and cultivates self-protection, which in turn fosters growth.

I believe we all negotiate way too much. We negotiate our jobs, our relationships, our boundaries, our time, our passions, our health, and our happiness. It happens gradually. We don't wake up one day and decide to compromise our lives. We do it a little here, a little there. Life forces us to bend. We want to be kind and we want others to like us. Then one day we wake up and realize that there's nothing left to compromise. We've negotiated everything, and then we wonder why we're not happy.

Without non-negotiables, you can easily lose your sense of self. And if you don't know who you are, how will you know where you're going? You become aimless, lost, and stagnant—and that's when you drift into abusive relationships, fall into depression, cope with stress in unhealthy ways, and start to believe that you are worthless. Once you believe that you have no value, everything will be a compromise.

So how do you form non-negotiables? Well, look back at your life. Think about all the things that went wrong because you negotiated something. Follow that string and you will see that it's tied to your sense of self-worth, which is tied to your truth. You negotiated because you separated the two. Bad or unhealthy events always chase compromised truth.

> You cannot build a dream on a foundation of sand.
> To weather the test of storms, it must be cemented
> in the heart with uncompromising conviction.
> —T. F. Hodge

Okay, forget about the past. Let's talk about today with a first round of questions. What are you negotiating in your life right now? What are you negotiating in your career, and in your relationships with friends and family? Are you negotiating your health or your passions? Are you negotiating your desire to be heard, or how you want to be treated? Are you negotiating what you really want to do with your life?

Once you've considered the answers, think about this second round of questions. How does negotiating these things affect your state of mind, your well-being, your experience of life day-to-day, and your life overall? Think about it and play it out.

Finally, if you didn't negotiate these things, how would your life be different? Would you still be at your job? Would you still be in your current relationships or would you have new ones? Would you look and feel the same? Would your relationship with your family be different? What about your relationship with yourself? Just chew on this for now. You'll do a non-negotiable exercise later.

Now let's talk about resistance. As you create your non-negotiables, you will most likely feel some pushback. For example, say you decide that your new non-negotiable is to be in only healthy relationships. Period. You will no longer be in any relationship that you believe isn't healthy or good for you, no matter how strong the "chemistry" or attraction is. You may be resistant to letting go because it may mean that you will be alone. For some, being alone is almost as painful as being in an unhealthy relationship. So there's resistance—certain emotional obstacles that make it difficult for you to actually realize your non-negotiable. You may find yourself compromising, then the next thing you know you're once again involved in something that isn't healthy.

At the end of the day, it's all going to come down to what's at stake if you don't hold on to your non-negotiables. That's the question you should ask yourself. Using the example above, what's at stake if you negotiate being in a healthy relationship? Well, there's a high chance that you'll repeat toxic or unhealthy patterns. Your growth, potential, and happiness are at stake.

So let's start thinking about your non-negotiables. Here are a few of mine:

I will do my best to be a good father.

My father is an alcoholic. This means that at some point in his life, his addiction stunted his emotional growth. He did an excellent job providing basic things for his family: food, water, shelter, and designer clothes. But he did not provide much of an ear, empathy, or most importantly, presence.

One day I asked my father if I could buy a model plane from our neighbor, a pudgy man who sold toys out of his garage. His "hobby shop" was stocked with three hundred dollar remote-control cars and airplane models that required hundreds of intricate balsa wood pieces and a degree from M.I.T. But for an eleven-year-old with an obsession for Legos, it was just another play session and, hopefully, an excuse to spend some quality time with Pops. My father gave me the cash and I bought the plane. He took one look at it and laughed. He said there was no way that I could build it. Then he went back to clipping his toenails and reading *The Korea Times*.

I started building. Three hours later, my dad was snoring and I was sitting in front of what looked like a pile of popsicle sticks glued together. My dad woke up before I had time to hide my failure. He shook his head and said, "I told you."

We Remember Moments Like These. They form our beliefs. This is why I have the non-negotiable above.

I will not associate with anyone who assassinates my character.

John Gottman, a professor emeritus in psychology known for his work on marital stability and relationship analysis, predicted divorce at a 94 percent accuracy rate. He wasn't concerned about how many times a couple fought but rather *how* they fought. Assassinating your partner's character was a sure sign the relationship was doomed.

If you assassinate one's character, you are not fighting fair. You are using a gun instead of gloves. Simply put, you are being a bully. Bullies react from fear and operate from a false self, one driven by ego and approval. They don't have the tools to support or encourage your growth. Instead, they will ride your coattails and bring you down so that they can feel better about themselves. I have enough weight to carry. I do not need more dead weight.

I will do my best to make my partner feel beautiful.

In CrossFit, RX means prescribed. It's the recommended weight/ standard for one's workout. This is not about raising the bar— rather, it's the minimum requirement to do the workout as prescribed. Many do not RX (load the recommended weights or execute the recommended standard on the movements) because they are not physically able, which is understandable. But if you don't do it because you don't want to push yourself, that's called being lazy. Everyone that does CrossFit knows this. The coaches remind us daily.

In relationships, the RX I have set for myself is to do my best to make my partner feel beautiful. I have not done this in the past because it requires time and effort, and I was lazy. Being lazy is not acceptable to me anymore in any area, including my relationships. Being faithful and remembering birthdays is not enough. I don't just want to be great at work or in the box; I want to be a great boyfriend/husband. Making my girlfriend/wife feel beautiful is non-negotiable for me—it is my new RX.

I will walk with mirrors (not literally).

I believe that men walk with mirrors and boys do not. To walk with mirrors means to be aware of your defects and to be willing to change them. Think about all the men you have come into contact with in your life: fathers, brothers, grandfathers, teachers, or uncles.

- How many of them were exceptional men?

- How many of them led by example?

- How many had the ability to create safe spaces?

- How many admitted when they were wrong and shut up when they were right?

- How many changed your life?

If I asked myself how many real men I have experienced in the forty plus years that I have been on this planet, I would have trouble coming up with names. That's because we live in a fatherless nation. Dad is absent, either physically or emotionally, which leaves boys growing up confused and without a role model (like me). Then, as adults, we have unhealthy relationships and cause a lot of emotional destruction of our own.

I refuse to be a boy. I've been one for most of my life. One cannot be transparent without self-examination. Without transparency, growth is impossible—and growth is not something I am willing to negotiate.

> [The idea that] Father is someone who works hard, who isn't around much, who criticizes more than he compliments, who doesn't show affection or any other emotion except anger—no longer applies.[7]
> —John M. Gottman

I will have a cause.

I believe that everyone should have something that they are fighting for. It doesn't have to be solving world hunger. It simply means having a direction and a driving passion behind a cause you believe in with every fiber of your being. Without direction, there's no journey and no mission. You're a river, not an ocean. The ocean is where you find life.

A CAUSE CREATES LIFE.

I will not let my work determine my worth.

We often make a living at the expense of having a life. From early on, we've been programed to desire to be successful by peers, parents, teachers, society, and the media. We plan everything around that success: We study our asses off to get into top schools, and we sacrifice time, sleep, and relationships to climb the corporate ladder. Our definition of success becomes more and more narrow, until we forget that a big part of success is quality of life. When we finally reach the mountaintop, our heads are in the clouds. There is no view, only less air.

I used to determine my value by what I accomplished, and tied success directly to my self-worth. My value came in the form of a sale. At one point that value was determined by selling scripts, then drinks (when I ran the family business). By defining my sense of self-worth through what I sold, I sold myself. I became powerless. I was not human; I was a robot. This contributed to my unhappiness, as well as to the expiration of my marriage. I will never let that happen again.

I will take care of myself first.

I will not be able to help others if I cannot take care of myself. If I want to continue my cause—coaching others—I cannot negotiate my own self-care.

I will always have non-negotiables.

My non-negotiables are what make me who I am today and define my character. They give me value and a Stance. Without protection, I am exposed to everything that has taken me down a path that strips me of my potential.

MODEL IN A BOTTLE DOT-COM

At one time in my life, people thought that I was a pimp—literally. When I was in my late twenties, I had an idea: to create an Internet reality show about models that didn't have nudity, just real working models in Los Angeles. Streaming video had just been introduced to the world and there were no modeling shows on television at the time. This was pre-"America's Top Model."

But Modelinabottle.com failed miserably because I was negotiable. I had an investor who believed in me and gave me $100K to launch it. I rented a million dollar penthouse on The Sunset Strip and gave six models free rent in exchange for the ability to document their lives, castings, photo shoots, daily routines at the penthouse, etc. They ended up walking all over me. Or, more accurately, I allowed them to do so because I had no Stance. The penthouse became a frat house; the models brought in their boyfriends and had parties. They ditched the camera and were never home to chat with fans. Eventually, the owner of the penthouse terminated the lease because she thought that I was running a high-class escort service.

Here's what I negotiated:

- My friendship: My investor was also a friend. He trusted me with his money and I negotiated it for approval from others.

- My relationships: I pressured my girlfriend at the time to ask her agency (she was also modeling at the time) to connect me with talent. By doing this, I was willing to negotiate her reputation and career, as well as our relationship.

- My character: Allowing the talent to not follow the rules and act inappropriately gave off the impression that the person behind this project—me—was filming an episode of "Girls Gone Wild." I was portrayed as a soft-core porn producer and I was willing to negotiate that for a chance to jump on the Internet gold rush at the time.

- My gifts: Let's face it—I didn't go to film school to produce a modeling show. I did not have a genuine passion for the modeling business. I negotiated my talents for an image of success. In a nutshell, I sold out.

Would Modelinabottle.com have been a successful business if I'd had non-negotiables? I don't know. Okay, probably not. But I do know that I wasn't ready for success because I had no Stance. And part of having a strong Stance is having non-negotiables. Success in that world would have only encouraged me to be more negotiable, which would have meant getting further away from knowing who I was. With that kind of success and power, everything would have been negotiable to me, including my friends, my family, and myself. I believe this happens to many lottery winners who do not have a Stance. When you don't have a Stance, you make decisions based on your Pseudo Self.

RELATIONSHIPS MEAN COMPROMISE, NOT COMPROMISING SELF.

When you have non-negotiables, you create a shield. This doesn't mean that you create distance. Having non-negotiatbles should actually bring two people closer together in a healthy way. Instead of two people losing themselves in each other, we can have two individuals choosing to live life together. When you have a Stance, you protect yourself as well as your character, which means you bring more value to the table.

PRACTICE
Non-Negotiables

Make a list of all the things that you have negotiated about yourself that have led to poor and unhealthy decisions. Then write down the consequences of those actions.

Now make a new list. From everything you've learned thus far, what new non-negotiables do you want to create? What are you negotiating in your life right now in your relationships: parents, friends, partners, yourself? What about at work? Do you even have any non-negotiables?

Write down your new non-negotiables.

Then ask yourself: Why did you decide that these are the things you are no longer willing to negotiate? Write that down.

Finally, if you didn't negotiate these things, how would your life be different? Would you still be at your job? Would you still be in your current relationships or would you have new ones? Would you look and feel the same? Would your relationship with your family be different? What about your relations with yourself?

What you have in front of you is a map. Hold onto these non-negotiables and you will start to build the framework of your new container.

THE DAY I DIDN'T FIT IN

After working for four years for a nonprofit organization, I was ecstatic when I was hired to be a program director of a private treatment center for eating disorders. This was a chance of a lifetime. It meant I would hire my own team of therapists and spearhead my own treatment center. It also meant free yoga and a personal chef. It felt too good to be true. As it turned out, it was.

After three weeks, they told me I "wasn't a good fit."

This is the actual post from my blog the day I was terminated from a high-end treatment center:

I feel scared, confused, and disposable. I want to believe that what happened today is a test to see how much I've grown. I want to believe things are meant. No what-ifs, only what is. I feel like I'm on a balance beam, wind trying to shake me but I'm holding on tightly, not with my hands but only my Stance. My legs are frozen, numb, in shock, and I hope that I feel them soon. I trust that they will propel me forward. I feel that if I don't move forward, I am nothing. I am a lie, a puppet, a pumped out product with a generic label stamped on my forehead. The thought makes me feel nauseous and cheap. I left the house because I just had to go. Anywhere.

I got on my motorcycle even though there is a chance of rain. Let it rain. Let it pour. It will make me feel alive. I need that tonight. I came to the nearest Wi-Fi coffee shop. I feel safe here, like it's the home base tree. I parked in a car space, then got back on my bike and rode up the sidewalk and parked right in front. Someone yelled, "Fuck yeah." It made my heart smile. I felt like Batman inside my flat black helmet. I don't care. Give me a fucking ticket. This is me. I am here. Armed only with a computer stained with palm marks, I find a seat in the corner. Then I shrink.

I've been here before, in this state of mind, one filled with desperation, a slippery well. My sweatshirt tightens and I feel dehydrated like I did years ago when I was writing screenplays in coffee shops all day. I take a sip of my warm coffee, wanting to rip out of my skin because this is a coffin and I can't do it again. I can't. I won't. This place is fucking lonely and miserable, a hamster wheel. Now I question everything. Maybe I'm spinning on one already and don't know it.

Suddenly, I am concerned about the rain, worried I'm going to get a ticket. I look down at my helmet and realize it's just a helmet. Then I look up to see that I got a note on this post. One note from a follower on my blog. It says, "You are not alone." These four words snap me back, reminding me it's different this time. There are no what-ifs because I am not writing this to be someone. Only what is. I am writing this as someone. That is the difference. Suddenly I can feel my legs. They feel strong like the steel in my boots.

In fact, I was let go without explanation. The residential center I was supposed to run wasn't even up yet. I was *training* at one of the other treatment centers until my boss's licensing came through. Residential, outpatient, and transitional living were all owned by one person, who had spent the last twenty-five years building her empire. I was impressed by her ambition and work ethic but didn't believe in what she built: a well-oiled machine pumping out treatment as if it came in cans on a factory belt.

| Those who follow the crowd usually get lost in it.
  —Rich Warren

When someone gets let go or fired, the first feeling is usually panic: *How am I going to pay my bills? How am I going to pay for food and rent?* After logic kicks your ass, your emotional side takes over. You begin to internalize what happened and judge yourself: *Maybe I'm not good enough. Maybe I deserve to be fired. Maybe I should find a new career. I am worthless. I am stupid.*

But if you've worked your transparency muscles, you will:

- Fight your Pseudo Self (live your truth).

All the thoughts that label you as worthless, stupid, or incompetent come from your Pseudo Self. You need to be aware of this and remind yourself that they are only feelings (many of which stem from false beliefs you've internalized), and you are not what you feel. Accept that the event has made you sad, but understand that being let go does not define your worth.

- Live in healthy time (in the here and now).

You will not think about the past, reviewing the days you worked there and what you could have or should have done. You will not worry about the future: *What am I going to do now? How am*

I going to pay my bills? What are my friends going to think of me? Instead, you will live in the here-and-now. Accept what you feel and be present in it. If you need to cry, cry. If you need to yell, scream, or throw a chair, so be it. This is how you feel. This is where you are. For me, I needed to park my motorcycle on the sidewalk and blog.

- Don't own it (your experiences/events are not yours to control).

You will choose to believe that you were meant to be at that job for the exact amount of time that you were. Like a pair of bowling shoes, that job was borrowed and it was time to return it for someone else to use.

- Share your story (give instead of take).

One day you will be able to use this story to help someone going through similar challenges. Your story will become a prism as you share it with others, which will make your story bigger than you.

Scroll through your non-negotiables. One of mine helped me reframe the situation almost instantly, lifting anxiety right off my shoulders as if it were on wires. It was this:

I will not work for anyone who doesn't allow me to be me and/or doesn't respect me or my gifts.

I didn't know this at the time, but looking back I've learned that being let go was a blessing in disguise. I was let go because I didn't fit in—which, in this context, involved conforming and muting my true self. This would have kept me in a very pseudo state, not allowing me to create. I wouldn't have had the space to paint outside the lines—to play, learn, fail, and learn more. That is the only path that would have lead me to building my own team and life-coaching course. The Catalyst Course and later SHFT would have never happened if I'd kept my tie on and my mouth shut.

> Your time is limited, so don't waste it living someone else's life.
> Don't be trapped by dogma, which is living the result of other
> people's thinking. Don't let the noise of other opinions drown your
> own inner voice.
> —Steve Jobs

I don't want work to feel like a factory; I want it to feel like a canvas. I want to paint, invent, and create. My former boss did not allow that, and it's now become a non-negotiable for me. Additionally, the way my former boss let me go demonstrated a lack of respect for me as a clinician and a person. She didn't let me go personally: she had her accountant do it for her. Presented to me like a weather forecast, it felt cold and left no room for conversation. Having room for conversation is also now a non-negotiable for me.

After a few weeks, the sting wore off and I got very clear on what my new non-negotiables would be: I will only work for someone who allows me to swim, practice my gifts, and lets me be my Solid Self. In this regard, being let go was a gift; there was nothing to be upset about. The job would have led me into a dark cul-de-sac where I would have been robbed of my growth and potential.

I'm not telling anyone to quit their jobs because they feel like they're negotiating themselves. Many feel that way; actually, most of us do. That's just the world we live in. And unfortunately, we are not all in situations where we can hold onto our non-negotiables and move on to pursue careers for which we only have pure passion. But know that your compromises are made for a longer-term gain that's aligned with bigger (more authentic) aspirations. And maybe *that* can be your non-negotiable: having a sense of purpose and knowing that you are on a path will give you a stronger Stance, which will position you for what's to come.

THE DIFFERENCE BETWEEN DIGNITY AND PRIDE IS THAT ONE STEMS FROM EGO, THE OTHER FROM YOUR STANCE.

TRUE STORY

FADE IN:

INT. CHINESE RESTAURANT - NIGHT

JOHN KIM sits by the window alone reading *Linchpin* as he finishes his last dim sum when the WAITRESS approaches.

> WAITRESS
> How're you doing?

John looks up at her, deadpan.

> JOHN
> You know what?

She instantly looks nervous.

> JOHN
> You've been asking people that all day.
> So, maybe I should ask you how you're doing?
> She looks a bit shocked, confused, taken back.
> She fumbles her words…

> WAITRESS
> Um... fine, tired. Been here since 10 a.m.
> I can't wait to go home.

> JOHN
> I bet.

She smiles.

> WAITRESS
> Thank you.

She needed that.

> JOHN
> You're welcome.

> WAITRESS
> (extra friendly)
> Would you like anything else?

> JOHN
> No, I'm good. Just the check. Thank you.

She grabs the check from her apron, sets it on the table with a fortune cookie on top, smiles, and leaves.

John grabs the fortune cookie and cracks it. He reads his fortune, looks out the window.

His eyes get glassy.

He really needed that, especially this week, since he was let go from his job.

He turns back to the fortune, snaps a picture of it with his phone.

FADE OUT:

Perspective changes everything. You can feel hopeless and discouraged one minute, then hopeful and blessed the next, just by changing your perspective. A simple example of this is when we see or hear about a great tragedy: 9/11, Hurricane Katrina, the earthquake that swallowed Japan. Suddenly, your partner leaving his socks on the couch isn't that big of a deal. Your boss is tolerable. The bills are just bills. At least you have your health. Only your perspective shifted.

Stance can help change your perspective by providing you with new lenses to look through. They can be simple, fun, and something you hold on to just for yourself.

FUCK IT FRIDAY!

For me, *Fuck It Friday!* means a donut. I have a weakness for them. I know they are bad for me, but every Friday I allow myself one. By allowing myself a treat every once in a while, I'm telling myself that everything doesn't have to be black and white or cut-and-dried. Rewards are okay; I can fudge. As a matter of fact, I must. It's healthy.

It doesn't matter if it's food, an experience, a massage, a workshop, a trip, an affirmation, a compliment, or a day off. You need it—not the reward, but the ability to give yourself something you deserve without feeling guilt. The process of allowing yourself to receive is crucial. You are validating your worth. Many of us struggle with this. Instead, we focus solely on others for validation. Having a Stance means learning how to validate yourself. This is an important tool when you begin to build yourself a safe container, which we'll address in the following chapter.

Having a Stance also means taking back what you've lost: knitting, skating, writing, jumping on trampolines—what used to make you forget? What brought you joy? Take it back. So many of us lose what once made us happy in the daily grind of life. It becomes the project car sitting on blocks and collecting dust in the garage. It's time to take the cover off and get back to building, discovering, learning, creating—whatever it was that made you lose track of time.

For me, it wasn't writing screenplays—it was the process of giving birth to ideas. It started in childhood with building with

Legos. I used to lock myself in my room for hours and get lost in my creations. It's always been there. After I quit screenwriting, I lost that part of me. I stopped conceiving and a piece of me died.

UNLOCK YOUR CODE

Sometimes growth is more about a reunion than anything else. I believe that at some point in our life, usually when we're young, something happens that forces us to grow up fast and become an "adult." We stuff that part of us that holds what we really love into a hope chest and lock it. Maybe it was when your parents got a divorce, or when your brother got sick and you had to take care of him. Maybe it was the expiration of a toxic relationship that left you alone and having to start all over again.

Whatever it was, some or many events in your life caused a separation with self. We're then slowly shaped by external elements: parents, family, expectations, advertising, social pressures, bills. We start living from the outside in, instead of from the inside out. We allow everything external to affect our decisions and the way we think. Unlocking your code means taking the person we stuffed into a hope chest back out and giving her a voice again. It's inside-out living, not outside-in living. The difference is feeling power-filled instead of powerless.

I stopped going to coffee shops after I quit screenwriting. This was the actual blog post I wrote the day I stepped back into one to write again:

"Surf your balls off," she replies casually, as if she's reminding me my shoes are untied. I chuckle on the inside as I plop down at my table and punch those exact words into the passcode box for free wireless. I am back in the corner of a coffee shop today. This time, answering client emails and questions from my blog, hoping to ignite a change in the way one thinks.

Everything's the same. The cheap coffee, the bad art, the starlet whipping foam mechanically behind the counter, and the sea of struggling screenwriters typing with urgency that will only last a few minutes before they, too, become robots. I guess the only difference between now and five years ago, besides the amount of grass in my hair and change in my pocket, is who I'm typing for.

Before, it was for me, my life, my future. Now, it's for others, their life, and their future. I am not saying that I have the ability to help anyone. I am just saying that is my intent. I ponder this and realize that this small difference—the intent to do something for someone else instead of yourself—creates a bulletproof sense of productivity because you can't fail when you give.

They may still not like what I have to say, but they can't argue with my heart. I am still writing on spec, as they say in Hollywood. Before, the speculation that my story is viable. Today, the speculation that your story is valuable. This makes me happy. I take a deep breath and smile, angled on a wooden chair with my back against the wall like I used to sit for hours years ago, realizing that I can take this place back. I feel comfortable here. I feel safe. It's my tree house.

It wasn't until I started a blog that I began to take things back. I didn't realize it at the time. I didn't say to myself: *I need to take things back that I once loved doing.* I created a blog because I wanted to connect, but inside the itch to create was surfacing again. The blog just happened to be the tool I used. Creating allowed me to connect not only with others, but with myself. That is the important piece: Whatever you decide to take back will allow you to connect with yourself.

> To me, punk rock is the freedom to create, freedom to be successful, freedom to not be successful, freedom to be who you are. It's freedom.
> —Patti Smith

What's keeping you from living inside-out instead of outside-in is fear. You are afraid that by unlocking your inner code, you will not be what you *should* be, or who you *should* be. You're afraid of showing your true self because people may not like it. You're afraid to rock the boat, to get out of your comfort zone. You are afraid of the unknown. You're afraid that you may actually be powerful.

Unlocking your code and allowing your true self to emerge often involves being different, and being different is terrifying. I get it. But you will never be who you were meant to be if you don't tap into that part of you. Think of it this way: If you don't unlock your inner code, you will always be incomplete. To be whole—to be completely you—you need to unlock your inner code, rip off whatever muzzle you strapped on yourself years ago, and tap into your potential.

Here's another example from my own life: I used to get lost in breakdancing when I was around ten. I would do it every day after school for hours. I liked myself when I was breakdancing and the lifestyle became a part of me. Now, unlocking my inner code doesn't mean that I'm going to start breakdancing and tagging walls as a forty-two-year-old man. Or it could, I guess. But in my case, it's about reuniting with the spirit of that ten-year-old: giving him a voice and starting a relationship with that true version of me that I locked away years ago.

Lately, that part of me comes out to play when I'm in the CrossFit box, riding my motorcycle, and doing other things that connect me to that spirit. This connection makes me feel alive. So what part of you did you lock up when life happened? What part of you did circumstances compel you to ignore? Many of us had to become parents or take care of our siblings because our parents weren't able to. What would it look like to listen to that part of you that you had to turn away from? When I ask what would it look like, I mean: What action steps can you apply to your life to create this reunion?

Growth is about finding the right combination to the lock that's keeping you from who you really are.

> [T]he "acorn theory" ... holds that each person bears a uniqueness that asks to be lived and that is already present before it can be lived.
> —James Hillman

PRACTICE

Unlocking Your Code

Explore what you gravitate toward and rediscover what moves you. You can't move forward, evolve, and grow, if you don't allow yourself to flourish. Identify and reconnect to the spirit you were born with. Ask yourself: What part of you have you been ignoring? What part did you stuff into a hope chest when shit went down? Really try to tap into the spirit of that person. Open the hope chest and pull her out. What's the first thing she says to you? Write that down.

What would it look like if you were to have a relationship with this person? How would that manifest in your everyday life?

What action steps would you need to take if you were to start listening to and addressing your old/new self?

Having a Stance means unlocking your code and reuniting with those parts of yourself that you've ignored.

> A self is not something static, tied up in a pretty parcel and handed to the child, finished and complete. A self is always becoming.
> —Madeleine L'Engle

And sometimes "becoming" means reuniting.

SEEK AND STRETCH YOUR NECTAR

Someone once told me: *Life is shit except for a few moments of joy.* If that's the case, we must stretch those moments like cookie dough. Everyone has bright spots, though most of us are unaware of them. We are so busy obsessing about the future and dwelling on the past that we don't notice them. They fly by like our adolescence. We need to turn our dial from macro to micro and taste the nectar in our lives: the first sip of hot coffee in the morning, the few seconds after a brisk run, consuming your favorite meal, the scent of your lover, a life-changing conversation, feeling beautiful in a dress, the moment you forget that you're on a motorcycle.

Nectar is everything you enjoy right now in your life. It's not what you want or had. It's what you have right now, today. And if you don't believe that you have anything, you need to look harder. It's there; we all have nectar in our lives. But we don't all have the ability to produce it—and by "produce," I mean to seek and stretch. Producing nectar requires a certain mindset (and lots of practice) that starts first with a decision to put on a fresh lens and notice what brings you joy in life. Stretching that joy doesn't just mean to do more of it—it means being completely present while you're enjoying it.

> If while washing dishes, we think only of the cup of tea that awaits us, thus hurrying to get the dishes out of the way as if they were a nuisance, then we are not "washing the dishes to wash the dishes." What's more, we are not alive during the time we are washing the dishes. In fact we are completely incapable of realizing the miracle of life while standing at the sink. If we can't wash the dishes, chances are we won't be able to drink our tea either. While drinking the cup of tea, we will only be thinking of other things, barely aware of the cup in our hands. Thus, we are sucked away into the future—and we are incapable of actually living one minute of life.[8]
> —Thich Nhat Hanh

This quote really resonates with me. When I was going through the most difficult time in my life, I felt the most calm when I was doing the dishes. My life was out of control at the time, but I had control keeping the dishes clean, and maybe that made me feel a sense of calm. I don't know; maybe it was just the feeling of warm water on my hands and the gratification of cleaning something. I just remember that it always snapped me back into the present. The dishes got me through some hard times.

Today, I still hand-wash dishes when I need to reboot and get back to the here-and-now. I find that the fastest path to get to the present is through activities. I know meditation is technically an activity, but I'm referring to daily actions where joy and passion live. Meditation has always been difficult for me, because I've always defined it as sitting lotus-style on a cushion, and I struggle with sitting still. But you don't have to sit to meditate. You can meditate while you're moving: while you're riding a motorcycle, walking to work, and yeah, hand-washing dishes. On a basic level, meditation involves tapping into the here-and-now, and one way to do that is to seek and stretch your nectar. There is an undeniable correlation between nectar and being present. When we are doing activities that produce joy, we are the most present.

Only this actual moment is life.
–Thich Nhat Hahn

The more you're aware of all the nectar in your life, the more you're training your brain to appreciate the little things in life—the things you have today. If we stretch these moments and string them together, your days will feel happier, lighter, and you can flip the script and believe that:

LIFE IS JOY EXCEPT FOR A FEW MOMENTS OF SHIT.

Being aware of your nectar and stretching it is having a Stance.

PRACTICE
Seek and Stretch Your Nectar

I. What are the bright spots in your life right now? Don't just think about them, write them down. It's important for you to see them on paper. What brings you pure joy in your daily life? Not things you want or once had, but things you have right now, currently. It doesn't matter how big or small they are as long as they bring you joy.

Here's a snapshot of the nectar in my life currently.

- Motorcycle rides: when there's no traffic, beautiful weather, and everything is spontaneous. When I forget that I'm on a bike.

- CrossFit Wods (workout of the day): specifically, the twenty seconds of dopamine shooting into my brain after I've pushed myself beyond what I thought I could.

- Working with my team in the studio: the palpable synergy of many talented individuals coming together to execute one powerful vision.

- Juice: buying fresh vegetables and making juice in the morning. The feeling of healthy, fresh nourishment.

- Creating content: blogging, writing, and my new love for making raw unrehearsed videos.

- Spending time with friends: I used to enjoy deep long conversations, but these days, I enjoy light-hearted goofing around, with lots of room for laughter.

- Moments of meditation: when I am actually able to detach from my thoughts and linger in the here-and-now.

- Anchoring: through simple daily activities that help me practice being fully present.

- Breezes: anywhere, anytime. Something about wind on my face makes me feel like nothing matters.

There's nothing in this list that's dependent on accomplishing any big goal or obtaining a certain amount of money. They are things that I already have the ability to execute in my life. You don't seek nectar in what-ifs. You seek it in what is.

II. Now stretch your list. Again, make sure that they are things that you can execute today. If you love coffee, maybe the process of making coffee at home can be new nectar for you. Maybe you've always wanted to try salsa dancing or Jujitsu; maybe you've always wanted to switch up your yoga from regular yoga to hot yoga. Be creative. Explore. Stretch.

III. Write down the action steps to execute more new nectar in your life.

BE HEARD

The final piece in creating a Stance is about being heard, which is about expressing how you feel—not just your state-of-mind, but about things, opinions, perspective, your views on life. This isn't about preaching; it's about speaking your truth. There's a difference between someone who has an introverted personality and someone who doesn't allow herself to be heard. Most likely, it's a pattern that stems from childhood (or it could be something else). Either way, if you don't have the ability to be heard, you don't have a Stance. You are telling yourself that you don't exist or matter, and not allowing a vital part of yourself to live.

> Choosing with integrity means finding ways to speak up that honor your reality, the reality of others, and your willingness to meet in the center of that large field. It's hard sometimes.
> —Terry Tempest Williams

The way to be heard is to express how you feel, plain and simple. There's no other way. Many of us bottle up our feelings because we don't want to rock the boat; we misconstrue keeping quiet as being a nice person or a loving partner. But, in fact, this can turn into resentment and cause a shit-load of anxiety and other issues down the road.

> It is being honest about my pain that makes me invincible.
> —Nayyirah Waheed

Your feelings are like a pressure cooker, and you must release the valve. We need tools to avoid blowing a gasket, and many of us don't have them. I get it. Maybe our upbringings didn't provide us with space to exercise our self-expression muscles, so we grew up holding onto things not because we wanted to, but because we just didn't know any better. The more transparent you are, according to my definition of transparency, the easier it will be to release this valve.

One would think that self-expression should fall into the Transparency stage. While the act of telling someone how you feel is a form of transparency, what's really happening is that you are allowing yourself to be heard not just to others, but more importantly, to yourself. And that's the most important piece: being heard for your own sake, not for the sake of others. You are giving yourself a voice and proving to yourself that you exist. This process forces you to listen to yourself.

Many people don't listen to themselves. They have an inner dialogue going on, but they are not heard. If you are not heard, you become invisible. You are not there—or are you? This can't be a question. Put your hand down, and instead, stand, speak, teach, take over the class. It is imperative to do this not only in intimate relationships, but across the board, in all of your relationships: with your partner, family, friends, business partners, boss, co-workers, and yourself. Stating your position, even an emotional one, is part of your Stance.

HOW YOU FEEL IS YOUR TRUTH. IF YOU DON'T EXPRESS THAT, YOU ARE BEING FALSE.

Having a Stance means being heard.

PRACTICE
Be Heard

Where in your life do you feel unheard right now? In what relationships?

What do you feel unheard about?

What action steps can you take to make yourself be heard?

IN A SHOT GLASS
To create your Stance, you must:

- Have non-negotiables (things you are not willing to negotiate about yourself).

- Unlock your Inner Code (allow yourself to connect with that part of yourself that you locked away years ago).

- Stretch your nectar (enjoy more of the little things that bring you joy throughout the day).

- Be heard (listen to yourself by expressing yourself).

Chapter Four

Container

I believe that our emotional state, like our bodies, has the ability to heal itself as long as we provide it with a safe inner space— a container. Conversely, I believe that we prevent healing by creating unhealthy spaces—containers that invite harm. We then fall into the same dysfunctional patterns, retreat into our unhealthy coping habits, and get stuck in a cycle of suffering. Creating a safe container is the way out of that cycle.

OUR CONTAINER IS THE HEALTHY SPACE WE CREATE FOR OURSELVES WHERE GROWTH HAPPENS ORGANICALLY.

The key word is organic: growth that's fostered naturally. Many people believe that they need therapists and psychologists to grow. That is not true. We can't process everything by ourselves, but we don't need outside help to build a safe space for ourselves. We can build our own. And in that safe space, growth will happen.

Most of us have cracked containers from our stories and the shit we've been through. And when your container is cracked, your potential goes down. The chances of you achieving what you were meant to achieve—and affecting who you were meant to affect—diminishes significantly. Cracked containers allow dysfunction, which leads to anxiety, sucks away your motivation, and keeps you stuck in emotional quicksand. You're left going through the motions of life, but not really living. You become a grayed-out version of yourself.

It's time to build yourself a brand new container.

The word "container" came from my own story, and through exploring the various containers in my life: the residential treatment centers I worked at, the fraternity I joined, and the CrossFit box that changed my mind and body. Studying to become a marriage family therapist cemented the idea that growth happens in safe spaces, and that's what a therapist creates for you: a safe space. In that safe space, there is growth. I think in pictures and I loved the visual of each person having their own space or "container." It was an interesting way to describe the concept of growth.

So I began to wonder: What if we could create our own container? Is that possible? And if so, what would that look like? As I was going through my own winter, I started to apply on myself the therapeutic concepts I had used to help others. I practiced all the concepts mentioned thus far, including practicing Transparency and creating a Stance. The final piece was structure and a self-care plan, which we'll get into in a bit. With a new safe container, I began to grow naturally.

Before we delve more into the act of building yourself a new container, I want to pull the curtain back on my own story so that you can see the organic progress behind the concept.

MY OWN TREATMENT

My definition of a *therapist* used to be someone who looked like Dr. Drew: decked out in a freshly-pressed shirt and nursing a chai latte with one hand and a leather steering wheel with the other as he swings into a private treatment center somewhere in Malibu.

You can imagine my resistance when I accepted a job as an addiction counselor working with underprivileged teenagers in Los Angeles. As I mentioned in my preface, I had to wear a uniform: khaki pants and a golf shirt. I was also required to obtain a class B license in order to drive a 16-passenger van for Friday outings. I felt more like a camp counselor than a therapist. To top it off, the treatment model was "Therapeutic Community." They never taught us Therapeutic Community in grad school. It wasn't on the curriculum. It sounded old, from back in the day. And, as it turns out, it was.

The idea of people helping people dates back to the 1800s and is the core of 12-step meetings, correctional facilities, group homes, rehabs, and even fraternities. All of these are safe containers that promote growth, and all Therapeutic Communities can be safe containers. These safe environments facilitate change. The Therapeutic Community allows a person to grow by fostering an environment where people are valued and accepted. A strong sense of belonging to a nurturing community in an atmosphere of trust and security is a central tenet of the Therapeutic Community. It's based on the principle that the process of engaging with people who have similar struggles can be "treatment" in itself, as long as the group or container is safe. The process of going through something together creates a strong bond and promotes healing. It can also create conflict, but it's in this conflict that revelations are born. Remember, growth is fifty percent revelations and fifty percent execution, and the journey with the group cultivates revelations. The group then holds you accountable to execute your revelations.

Since the TC model didn't correspond to my notion of what a therapist looked like, I begrudgingly drove to the dilapidated two-bedroom house that was rumored to be haunted. I wasn't open to learning; I was closed off and frustrated, and I nearly quit—many times. But what kept me there were the kids and their stories: There was rape, drugs, self-mutilation, suicide attempts, 16-year-olds who had no desire to live anymore. Some were mandated into therapy by court; others literally had nowhere else to go. They were booted from foster care or had parents who wanted to pass them off like batons.

They also all had something in common. Besides their struggles with substance abuse, they came from fatherless homes. Their dads were out of the house or out of their minds. Most of the kids did not even know their fathers; others had fathers who were in prison. Being "older" and one of the only male therapists there, I felt how hungry they were for a positive male role model and a man who didn't want anything from them. The girls were standing too close. They didn't understand boundaries and wanted my attention. They saw me as a father figure or a sexual figure—or both. The boys were imitating me or challenging me. They saw me as the father they never had or the father they were so angry at. This created extreme discomfort and inner conflict. If I didn't have a Stance (non-negotiables), I would have left.

But because one of my non-negotiables is to be a good father one day, I knew that this experience would school me. Working with these kids transformed my non-negotiable into a fiery passion. The more I worked with them and their parents, the more I realized that I needed to be there. I accepted my position and leaned fully into it, and my heart started to open. I felt differently about the golf shirt and khakis: I embraced it. My uniform turned into a cape.

And so I stayed. For the next four years I would cook, play, laugh, cry—*do* life with these kids. I was completely oblivious to the fact that I was the one in treatment—"treatment" for the dysfunction created from the absence of my own father. My father was not a bad guy. He never hit me, which is curious for me to write since most people define unhealthy relationships as some type of physical abuse. But unhealthy comes in many forms: In my case, my father was emotionally absent and an alcoholic, so everything was about him. He also wasn't around much; he was always at work or out with his friends. There were no camping trips, no baseball games, no father-son life lessons or meaningful conversations that I could pass down to my own son. I remember a lot of logistical talk about business and what we needed to do to survive. He didn't live in the present much; everything was about the future.

I guess the apple doesn't fall from the tree, because this wired in me the same struggle with being present and finding happiness. I am constantly thinking about the future, which has caused riffs in my relationships. I was on the road to becoming my father until I started working with these kids. There is no doubt that the Therapeutic Community model works. It's the foundation of residential treatment and transitional living. Elements of it are found in 12-step meetings, which have helped millions, and even in a CrossFit box, which is why both communities are so powerful and have changed lives. In fact, I discovered CrossFit shortly after my divorce. I was eating frozen yogurt and feeling sorry for myself when I noticed what looked like an adult playground next door. It was lined with monkey bars, wall balls, and gymnastic rings. I strolled in to inquire and the next thing I knew, I was doing burpees for time.

I've never considered myself an athlete. I was on the football team in high school but never played. I was the kid with the whitest uniform and the kid the coach called in when there were seven seconds left in the game. I adapted to CrossFit movements fairly quickly. It may have been the breakdancing or skating in my past, but the bodyweight movements like pull-ups, push-ups, handstand push-ups, and muscle-ups came pretty naturally to me. I was keeping up with other CrossFitters who were athletes most of their lives. These were the guys on the field when I was on the bench, and this gave me motivation. I felt like I was a part of something, which made CrossFit fun.

The more time I spent at CrossFit, the deeper I got into the community. There is a difference between a CrossFit box and a commercial gym: One is a safe container and the other is not. A CrossFit box provides a space that allows members to get into each other's lives, support weaknesses, and challenge false beliefs.

It promotes growth and, as such, is a Therapeutic Community. A commercial gym does not provide this kind of space. Members check in, work out alone, and leave. CrossFit didn't just give me abs; it changed my life.

> No man is an island, entire of itself; every man is a piece of the continent, a part of the main.
> —John Donne

The idea that growth happens naturally in safe containers has been around since we discovered fire. If I look back on my life, I realize that I've been in Therapeutic Communities for most of it: The breakdancing crew when I was ten, a fraternity in college, residential treatment centers, CrossFit, my Angry Therapist online community, and now in a tech incubator creating SHFT. There is tremendous power in community. It's how we grow.

I can imagine you might have some questions. A few of these may be:

- Can you microbrew this model and apply it to yourself in everyday life?

- Can you have a safe container within yourself as well as the container of your community?

- Can there be smaller containers within bigger ones, and how would this expedite growth?

- Would your own container keep you safe from your bigger containers?

- Do you have to first have a safe container to reap the benefits of a greater one?

The answer to all the questions above is yes, or I wouldn't have written this book. It wasn't just work in residential that cemented this theory. Building a new safe container for myself while participating in other safe containers in my daily life proved to me that growth can be exponential and organic.

After you've practiced Transparency and created a Stance, the final part to building a safe container is structure.

STRUCTURE

Structure doesn't mean going to work, hitting the gym, eating dinner, watching TV, and going to sleep. That's called a schedule. Structure is not a schedule or a routine. It's a framework that keeps you balanced. We tend to underestimate how much maintaining balance contributes to living life successfully and productively. People tend to focus solely on work and the relationships they are in, and end up with lopsided lives. When your life is lopsided, you will not be at your optimal state.

> You will never feel truly satisfied by work
> until you are satisfied by life.
> —Heather Schuck

Structure stretches you and is the foundation of any safe container. The kids I was treating in residential ended up there because they did not have the tools to create a solid structure, but you do. You can think about your structure as a Self-Care Plan.

SELF-CARE PLAN

Most of us live unbalanced lives. We focus predominantly on our relationships, career, and money. But there are other areas of our lives that leave us feeling empty if we don't give them attention. We can't just eat meat at every meal without any vegetables, carbs, or fruit. Our potency lives in balance. Imagine a life equalizer: When the balance and frequency is right, the sound is crystal and you feel something. When it's off, it's just noise. Most people live unbalanced lives; their equalizers are off. Either there's too much bass or too much treble. Their life just feels like noise.

If you want to build a safe container that promotes growth, you must balance out your life by fulfilling your basic needs. Yes, basic needs. The following are not extra things for ourselves if or when we get to a certain place in our lives. We need to focus on these things right now. There are seven categories of basic needs: Emotional, Spiritual, Sexual, Financial, Physical, Intellectual, and Passion/Purpose. They are all the building blocks of your

Self-Care Plan. The more you meet your needs in each area, the safer your container will be.

EMOTIONAL

Let's start with the Emotional. Everyone needs a space to vent and process. For some, that space is created through friends and family. For others, a bathtub and a crossword puzzle, or coffee and conversation, or a power bar and a CrossFit box, or a webcam and a therapist can do the trick. As I mentioned earlier, if we don't allow ourselves to be heard—to express our truth (and part of our truth is how we feel)—we are turning ourselves into a pressure cooker, because suppressing or avoiding your emotions will only make them stronger. For example, if you're angry with your partner, you might try to distract yourself from feeling that anger, but it's still in there, brewing, growing like a virus, and darkening with resentment. Then, when your partner does something to upset you, you explode. This is your body's way of releasing your pent-up emotions.

Just as emotion suppression is your body's way of protecting you during a trauma, emotion release in a nontraumatic situation is your body's way of protecting itself from further damage. When something traumatic happens to you, you go into fight or flight—survival mode. Your emotions take a backseat so that you can do what's necessary to protect yourself. But it doesn't mean that those emotions go away: They just get suppressed or carry over like roll-over minutes on your cell phone plan. When we consistently suppress our emotions, we increase physical stress on our bodies as well as our blood pressure and the chance of diabetes and heart disease. Our joints stiffen and our bones weaken. Our immune system becomes more vulnerable, which then fosters more illness. For many, old chronic physical pain is, in fact, just the body storing old repressed emotional shit. In order to live a healthy, free life, you must create spaces to release your emotions.

> Your emotions are the slaves to your thoughts, and you are the slave to your emotions.
> —Elizabeth Gilbert

SPIRITUAL

Getting in touch with your spirituality doesn't mean that you have to be religious or attend church. It just means that you believe in something greater than yourself. It doesn't matter if it's God, the universe, or aliens. Having this mindset allows us to surrender, accept, and let go. Sometimes our ego acts as a barrier to healing, but if you believe that you are a part of something bigger, the ego diminishes. It's much easier to "lose" when you're on a team than if you're playing solo.

> Spirituality does two things for you. One, you are forced to become more selfless, two, you trust to providence.
> —Imran Khan

> Happiness cannot be traveled to, owned, earned, worn, or consumed. Happiness is the spiritual experience of living every minute with love, grace, and gratitude.
> —Denis Waitley

> Just as a candle cannot burn without fire, men cannot live without a spiritual life.
> —Buddha

Tapping into something greater than yourself is extremely powerful. You can live a "through me" life instead of a "to me" life. "To me" is when we believe we are victims. Everything happens to me; it's the most powerless state. "Through me" is the most powerful state. In this state, you allow yourself to be more of a vessel. Something greater works through you, motivating you to do what you were meant to do on this planet. This is when fear dissipates, purpose is found, and your gifts shine. And it's easier to tap into this state when you have a spiritual life.

Now, spiritual doesn't mean religious, and going to church every Sunday doesn't necessarily make you a spiritual person. Spirituality is having a connection with anything greater than yourself and your ego: God, the universe, the moon, whatever you feel a connection to that serves a greater purpose than you.

Having this connection pulls you out of your own thoughts and story where fear and anxiety live. Spiritual experiences come in all forms and contexts: You can experience them in nature, surfing, fitness, meditation, yoga, etc. Some of my greatest spiritual experiences happen while I'm running life groups. I've had so many moments in this context when I've felt a greater power working through me. I learned to trust that power and became fearless, and that's when I shined the brightest.

WHEN YOU DON'T MAKE IT ABOUT YOU, THE UNIVERSE WILL.

How do you fulfill your spiritual needs? What do you do/where do you go to connect with something greater than you? The more you have a relationship with this greater power/energy, the more power/energy you will have when dealing with your own "problems."

> The spiritual quest is not some added benefit to our life, something you embark on if you have the time and inclination. We are spiritual beings on an earthly journey. Our spirituality makes up our beingness. —John Bradshaw

PHYSICAL

Moving your body should not just be something you do if you have extra time or motivation. It's a need—like sleep, water, and air. We are meant to move, not to sit in cubicles all day. We used to hunt our own food, swim, run, play, build things with our bare hands. Today, we spend most of our lives in bubbles: cars, offices, elevators, homes, and mostly in our heads. Our bodies become weak and we start to feel old. Without movement, we deteriorate and disconnect from our bodies.

Dancing, yoga, hiking, running, walking, biking, martial arts, surfing–anything that gets you out of the house and into your body is working out. It's a natural way to reduce stress and build self-esteem. Daily sweat rejuvenates the body and breathes life into our lungs. It gives us a sense of empowerment and is the fastest way to raise self-esteem. Yes, physical activity is a need. If you don't have a form of it in your life, your life is unbalanced. It's imperative to thread some sort of physical activity into your everyday life if you want to build a healthy, happy one.

> The human body is the best picture of the human soul.
> —Ludwig Wittgenstein

SEXUAL

We are sexual beings. If you deny that, then you are denying a part of yourself. But satisfying your sexual needs isn't about having a lot of sex; it's about feeling sexy and attractive, which is also the road to self-love and confidence. This can be done through anything: a new dress, salsa dancing, riding your motorcycle. But your sexy doesn't stem from anything external; your sexy comes from within. Clothes and activities might be an expression of that, but just because you look sexy doesn't mean that you feel sexy. So what is sexy? Sexy is courage, unapologetic laughter, certainty, love, humor, ambition, freedom, and comfort with self. At the end of the day, it is about an honest connection with self.

Most people attach sexy with their body, which is sold to us through messages in advertising—messages that we ultimately internalize. We forget that advertising is a production: It is made up, imagined, a lie. It's a trick we fall for daily. Instead of nurturing our inner truth, we work on the external things—body, clothes, makeup—and measure our sense of self-worth on society's standards of sexy. When we fall short, we internalize and stamp ourselves as not sexy and mute our Solid Self.

> I did not have a good self-image at first. Finally it occurred to me, I'm either going to love me or hate me… Confidence makes you sexy.
> —Queen Latifah

FINANCIAL

We need a roof over our head and food on the table. We need to pay our bills. Money is a very real thing and a legitimate need. Without it, we cannot fulfill many of our other basic needs. But fulfilling our financial needs isn't just about making money; it's about our relationship with money.

Most of us have a dysfunctional relationship with money. I know that I did. Lack of money management education paired with my impulsive personality has gotten me into personal debts, which has created anxiety and imbalance in my life. No one taught me the value of a buck or how to save when I was growing up. My parents were always at work, so they gave us spending money to entertain ourselves. We weren't rich but I always had money to buy junk food, clothes, go to movies, etc. Meanwhile, the other kids had to earn their money—they mowed lawns and ran paper routes—which forced them to establish a relationship with money.

As a young adult, whenever I bought food and spent money on entertainment, it didn't feel real. It felt like I was playing with Vegas poker chips. It wasn't until I got older and began to work that I began to establish a more honest relationship with money. I started to respect money because I knew what it took to make it. It also reflected in my grades. When I went back to school for my master's degree, I got straight A's (something I'd never achieved before) because I was paying for it myself. As a kid, I was enabled by my parents giving me spending money to buy things, which created a habit and trained my brain. As an adult, this became knee-jerk behavior. So I needed to develop a more healthy relationship with money and retrain my behavior/habits.

The thing about money is that you're never going to have enough. It's like an itch that gets worse if you scratch it. So you have to determine what is a financial need and what is an obsession. Your self-care plan is all about balancing your life, and your financial need is just one piece of the pie.

> Money is only a tool. It will take you wherever you wish,
> but it will not replace you as the driver.
> –Ayn Rand

Addressing your financial needs is about getting your money right, whatever that means to you. It's about having control over your finances so that your finances don't have control over you. Does money have control over you today? If so, how? In what way? How does this affect your state and life?

> Man makes the money. Money doesn't make the man.
> —LL Cool J

INTELLECTUAL

Once we leave school, many of us lose our learning habit. We get so caught up in our daily routine that we forget to take in anything new. Our brains go down the same tracks over and over. We need to cultivate our intellectual life and lay new tracks by feeding our brain new content regularly and challenging our minds. Like a muscle, the more we exercise our brain, the stronger it will get. This doesn't mean that we have to do long division and consume dense books. For me, "brain exercise" means digesting short blogs and lots of short videos, because I hate long-winded information. I can't sit in a classroom without daydreaming. My mind wanders very quickly, so I need things presented in a shot glass. Fortunately, the Internet is perfect for that, because it's the source of endless brain food. We no longer have any excuse not to feed our brain other than our own laziness. It doesn't matter how you feed your brain—through books, videos, whatever works. Just make sure that you feed it, or it will die.

> A mind needs books as a sword needs a whetstone,
> if it is to keep its edge.
> —George R.R. Martin

How do you digest information? What feeds your mind and inspires you? When I'm on the computer distracting myself from work, I try to watch videos that are intriguing and will teach me something new, enlighten me, and stimulate my mind. Without this intention, my hand will autoclick on pet tricks and breakdancing. Since I'm always on the computer, this intention manifests as a routine that allows me to stretch my brain and lay new tracks.

PASSION/PURPOSE

I talk to so many people who are frustrated because they haven't found their purpose. But purpose is not found, it's forged. It doesn't just fall into your lap. You have to design it and build it out, which takes effort, like anything of value in life. The greatest misconception about purpose is that you only have one. That puts a lot of pressure on you if you haven't found your purpose. And that pressure turns into anxiety and feeling lost in the world. Then we internalize that and start to believe that we have little or no worth.

The truth is we have multiple purposes. And our purposes change as we change and go through different chapters in our life. When I was a kid, I thought I was meant to dance. Then I thought I was meant to fly through the air on a skateboard. In my twenties, I thought I was supposed to move people through film. Today, I believe I'm supposed to help people through my words and ideas. Tomorrow, who knows. What's important isn't to know what your purpose is. What's important is the action of either exploring to find your purpose, or following what you think it might be. This process is what will paint your life.

Once you find your current purpose, know your why. This is what will give you traction as well as validate if your purpose is truly a purpose, or just something you're chasing for your own ego and self. Why are you doing what you do? Does it allow your unique gifts to shine? Does it line up with your story and who you are? Is it bigger than you? The stronger your why, the stronger your purpose. If you don't know why you're doing what you do, then you don't know your purpose.

> He who has a why to live for can bear almost any how.
> —Friedrich Nietzsche

Without a why, you will have no traction on which to build your purpose.

Start with this: What lights you up? What makes you lose track of time? What compels you to the point of obsession? What makes you want to go to sleep so you can do it again the next day? Follow that road—and by follow, I mean incorporate it into your life. Turn your passion into a verb and live it as much as possible. That requires effort, time, planning and, for many, breaking through your fears. But having a sense of purpose brings meaning to life and makes it three-dimensional. We won't feel complete if we are not living with a sense of purpose. It doesn't matter how much money you have: You will eventually feel empty without a sense of purpose. It is a basic human need. It's not about being happy; it's about fulfillment.

> The purpose of life is not to be happy. It is to be useful, to be honorable, to be compassionate, to have it make some difference that you have lived and lived well.
> —Ralph Waldo Emerson

If you don't have any strong whys, then ask yourself: What are you naturally good at? You know what it is—people keep telling you about it, but you dismiss it. You don't believe you can turn it into something great, or maybe you're afraid. Remember, your purpose doesn't have to be a single bell that you have to ring until you die. You can have many purposes in life that can change as you change. Exploring your purpose can be your purpose for now—that's okay. That may be a step in getting to your purpose, and a step is still moving forward; it's still moving toward your true north.

Once you have a Self-Care Plan, you will see what needs aren't being fulfilled and which might be overloaded. It will become your blueprint for building a structure that will help you fulfill and balance your needs. Your new structure should be designed to accommodate those needs that are not being fulfilled. For many, this will be their financial need, which is all about work. That said, I think we focus so much on our career that we forget about our deeper needs. We forget this one basic fact: WE ARE NOT WHAT WE DO.

Not fulfilling our basic needs keeps our lives lopsided, lowers our potential, and cracks our container. When we fulfill our basic needs, our lives organically become more balanced, whole and complete. Our state-of-mind starts to change, which then changes our thoughts and behaviors. And when our thoughts and behaviors change, our lives change.

PRACTICE: SELF-CARE PLAN
Write down what you're currently doing to meet your seven basic needs. They can overlap in categories. For example, working out is obviously a physical need, but it can also fall under a sexual need since it's an activity that can make you feel sexy.

Emotional
Spiritual
Physical
Sexual
Financial
Intellectual
Passion/Purpose

Notice where you are meeting your needs and where you are not. Notice which categories are sparse. Is there an imbalance?

Which categories need more fulfillment? Which are overloaded?

For the needs that require more attention, ask yourself: What is preventing you from fulfilling each need? Write down the barriers that get in the way of fulfilling each need.

For example:

I don't want to go back to a 9 to 5.
I'm afraid I'll fail.
I don't have enough time.
I'm broke.
I'm too lazy.
I don't want to drive twenty minutes to a class.
I don't have any motivation.

In the next month, give me a date when you will make a step toward fulfilling each need that still needs to be fulfilled. What is that first action step? Remember, it's just a step. It doesn't have to actually fulfill the need. Make sure you assign a date for each step, what need it's fulfilling, and why you want to accomplish this step.

For example:

March 15. Financial/Purpose: I will research blogs and online platforms where I can get published so that I can develop a social media following, grow an online practice, and make some $$!

March 20. Intellectual: I will wake up 30 minutes earlier and digest half an hour of online videos to educate myself on various wellness and personal growth topics to keep feeding my brain and learn more concepts.

April 1. Physical/Spiritual: I will go hiking once a week instead of doing CrossFit to both keep fit and get more in touch with nature.

April 15. Emotional/Spiritual: I will explore five meditation apps, join one, and meditate twenty minutes every single weekday, to calm my mind and explore my spirituality.

Your Self Care-Plan is a practice; you must integrate it into your daily life and grow it as you work on it. It's all about action/execution. Remember, growth is 50 percent revelations and 50 percent execution. Revelations alone aren't enough to produce change; we must apply what we know into a daily practice. Without a practice, growth and change are just ideas. Like a car without an engine, you won't go anywhere without a plan of action.

Everyone's practice will be different. You have to decide what yours will look like. Start small and focused. Pick one thing that you know you want to work on. Maybe it's your fitness and diet, or maybe it's learning to be a better listener. Maybe it's writing or exploring your passions. Have you had this conversation with yourself before? If so, what stopped you from moving forward? Most likely, fear is holding you back. If that's the case, maybe that should be your new non-negotiable: You will not allow fear to stop you from giving.

Once you have created your Self-Care Practice, tell people about it: Announce your change. Put it out there. Most people keep it private and there's no one to hold them accountable. So tell your friends and ask them to support you in your journey. Maybe they will create a Self-Care Practice as well and you can both make each other accountable.

Now practice Transparency:

- Fight your Pseudo Self (live your truth).

- Stop living your lies (pulling from your false beliefs).

- Live in healthy time (in the here and now).

- Don't own things that are not yours (let go).

- And accept and share your story (give instead of take).

Strengthen your Stance:

- Hold on to your non-negotiables (things you are not willing to negotiate about yourself).

- Unlock your inner code (allow yourself to connect with that part of you that you locked away years ago).

- Seek and stretch your nectar (enjoy more of the little things that bring you joy throughout the day).

- And be heard (listen to you by expressing yourself).

Practice Transparency and create your Stance daily and you will have three pistons pumping. You've almost built your container.

Now let's talk a little bit about friends and family.

YOUR TOP FIVE

Many years ago, a cell phone company did a promotion where you could add your top five friends to your plan. The slogan was, "Who's in your top five?" The ad featured five mugs circulating on the cell phone screen. I remember it because it made me question who would be in my "Top Five."

I didn't have many friends when I was married; I had a lot of acquaintances. That was back when I was running a restaurant bar in Hollywood and was surrounded by actors, producers, screenwriters, DJs, bartenders, and door guys. None of them were friends according to my definition of *friend* today. They were part of my social network and I spent a lot of time with them, but they did not contribute to my truth. Under the "friendship," there was a negotiation, an exchange. It was not announced or articulated; it was subconscious. I received approval and affirmation, and they received entrance into a club, a paycheck, free meals, and my approval and affirmation. We became a group of followers, a school of fish swimming in a bowl.

Here's what happens: In high school, we can't be picky. We don't have the tools. We are just discovering who we are. There's no way of knowing who will contribute to our growth because we don't know what growth looks like. Combine that with the force of peer pressure and our natural desire for acceptance and approval at that age, and friends become labels and the manner in which we identify ourselves: We are skaters, jocks, prom queens, band geeks, nerds, badasses—take your pick. It doesn't help that the educational system doesn't teach us about how to cultivate self-knowledge.

This social model sets us up for life. According to psychologist Erik Erikson's "Stages of Development," our basic strengths at this age are devotion and fidelity. Instead of finding ourselves in friends, we lose ourselves in them. Once in college, we start to form beliefs, ideas, and opinions that put us in a position to give instead of take. We have the tools we need to start looking for mutual, satisfying relationships, which means that we can slowly start to peel our labels off.

For many, this is make-up time—a chance to redeem what we missed in high school. Now that we've blossomed, we can be prom kings and queens, and this is where the road forks: If that "make-up time" never gets made up here—meaning we don't get our crown and realize that it's made of plastic—it carries on into our twenties. I believe this is when our Pseudo Self is the strongest. We posture, perform, and desperately try to prove ourselves to others, and can drift further from our Solid Self. That being said, I don't know if we have the desire or even the ability to pull exclusively from our Solid Self in our twenties. Our twenties are all about seeking and exploring, and that's okay. I actually encourage our Pseudo Self to dominate our twenties, since it's one way we learn about developing more authentic relationships with ourselves.

We must be aware of what might be preventing our growth. Back to those transparency muscles: The stronger they are, the easier it is to shed labels, de-mesh from our lovers, and attract friends who will call you out on your shit, support your strengths, challenge you, and completely accept you. Attracting those types of friends are crucial. You can't build a safe container by yourself or just with your partner. Like any Therapeutic Community, you are rebuilding yourself through others. Finding your Top Five is a crucial part of building your new container.

> A man's friendships are one of the best measures of his worth.
> —Charles Darwin

GREGSLIST

After my wife and I decided to separate, I went on Craigslist looking for a roommate. My new roommate was Greg, a single white gay male with exquisite taste in living spaces. I can feel his proud smile as I am typing this. A few months in, my wife and I decided to officially divorce, which left me with a roommate but no friends. My wife was my only friend, and I believe this was a contributing factor to our expiration.

I was in my mid-thirties at the time, and found myself having to start over again. It would not be easy this time—I had nothing to offer anyone. The club was gone and so were my connections. All that was left was a very broken boy in his thirties. The good news, which I would not discover until later, was that having nothing to offer but myself was an excellent filter to catch real friends. I guess you could say that Greg was a friend, but I didn't feel like I was on his list—I felt like he kept me from his other friends. In fact, I felt that high school thing happening all over again, and having just left the club world (which is the biggest high school thing of all), I found myself looking elsewhere. My search might have hurt his feelings (and if you're reading this Greg, now you know it was me, not you.)

I met a friend at church—the first Asian guy I had ever met who could actually grow a full beard. He was burly and crass, just like me. He introduced me to another friend—another Asian guy in his thirties who was divorced and studying to be a therapist. The similarities were uncanny: He was a former newscaster and I was a former screenwriter. We both felt like we were chasing the wrong rainbow and quit to become therapists. It was as if God said, *Hey John, I know you've never had any Asian friends, so let me give you a Chinese version of yourself.* Sam and I became roommates. Through Sam, I met another friend, my spiritual brother.

He had the same heart as me. We were both thirsty and search-
ing for a new definition of what it meant to be a man. Through
him I met a half Chinese/Hungarian guy with the same simian
palm lines as me going through a similar rebirth. That was freaky.
Then I met another friend—a war vet adjusting to life back in the
States. I called him my same-size brother because he was exactly
the same height and build.

Suddenly, I had a core or a "Top Five." We were all broken
men in our thirties, trying to figure out life. These people were
very different from the type of people I was used to spending
time with. They weren't actors, models, or club promoters. They
were just normal guys, and we had nothing to offer each other
except our stories.

So we began to do life together: Big Bear, coffee shops,
CrossFit, mountain bikes, walks around the lake, movies, din-
ners. We challenged and sharpened each other. They encouraged me to write again. After a five-year hiatus from writing,
I wrote a screenplay about my experiences with them. I didn't
write this script to sell it; it was just for me. It was a way to
unlock my code, to create again. My friends enjoyed the script
and encouraged me to go out and make it. With their support,
we began raising money to make it independently. Meanwhile,
the producer of the project encouraged me to create some silly
raw videos on the Internet as a marketing tool. That's when I
created *The Angry Therapist.*

Our paths are never how we imagine them to be. Life always
has other plans. Usually the unexpected is the road that leads us
to our purpose. In my case, getting stripped down to my essential
self and having to start all over by connecting to "real" people
who encouraged my Solid Self led me to create what's become
the center of my life today. The lesson is always the same: If you
stay true to your no-bullshit self, eventually life will take you
where you're supposed to go. All you have to do is hold on.

We are not meant to do life alone, and just because you have
a boyfriend, girlfriend, husband, or wife doesn't mean you're not
alone. We all need our own set of friends, whether we're in a relationship or not. We are inherently social creatures; we're meant to
learn from each other and strengthen each other. Without solid
healthy friends, we become dull swords.

It's time to put your friends in a strainer and spend more time with the ones who are going to encourage growth, not stunt it.

> Friendship is the hardest thing in the world to explain. It's not something you learn in school. But if you haven't learned the meaning of friendship, you really haven't learned anything.
> —Muhammad Ali

PRACTICE
Top Five

Here's your strainer:

- Friends who accept you and all your defects.
- Friends who believe in and support your journey.
- Friends who practice Transparency.
- Friends who have a Stance.
- Friends who see you as a part of *their* container.

Now, think about each one of your friends and put them through this strainer. Do they accept you and all your defects, or do they only accept you when it's convenient or under certain circumstances? Do they believe in and support your journey, or do they disagree with it and try to change your direction? Do they only support you when your path lines up with theirs? Do they practice Transparency or do they not show themselves to you? Do they have their own Stance or are they moldable depending on who they're around? Do they see you as a part of *their* container?

Which friends actually pass this test?

Remember, history alone doesn't give your friends a ticket to be in your top five. Many of us believe that just because we went to high school or college with someone, we have to be best friends with them for life. That's not true. People change and grow out of their friends—and that's okay. It doesn't mean that you have to cut these people out of your life, but they don't have to be in your Top Five. Your Top Five are the friends who accept, support, and protect you. They are the friends who will sharpen you.

The weaker your Transparency muscles and the less Stance you have, the more you will attract and be attracted to false friends, because you'll be operating from your Pseudo Self, not your Solid Self. The more work you put into Transparency and Stance, the tighter your strainer, which means the more you'll attract people who will encourage your growth, your path, and your truth.

THE OTHER F WORD

We've talked about friends and lovers. Now, let's talk briefly about family. The first thing to remember is that you cannot change your family. Instead, focus solely on being your Solid Self when you are interacting with your family members. This involves being transparent and holding onto your Stance, which can be extremely difficult among family. There will be an internal tug of war between who you were and who you are now—or who you want to be. When you are around your family, it's easy to snap back into the same family dynamics in which you grew up. That's why grown men, CEOs of giant corporations, regress into insecure teenagers when they're around their mothers. Although you may have changed, if your family hasn't changed you risk snapping back into the same dynamic you experienced growing up.

> Happiness is having a large, loving, caring, close-knit family in another city.
> −George Burns

I've gone through years of therapy and have come a long way. I'm not as reactive as I used to be: I think, process, and then respond. But even after my long road of personal growth, I am instantly triggered when I see my parents and become highly reactive. I know this about myself and try not to get sucked in, but the

dynamic is so strong that it's almost like I become possessed. This
is because they haven't changed at all. Old feelings float to the top,
all the work I've done on myself goes down the drain, and I turn
sixteen again. Of course, it's gotten better over the years as my
ability to pull from my Solid Self has gotten stronger and stronger.
But sticky family dynamics that stem from my early years are still
there and they are very powerful. I literally have to have a conversation with myself before seeing them and remind myself that they
are who they are, and that the only variable is me. I'm better able
to control myself and the things that come up from the past when
I do this. I'm able to be more patient, understanding, and loving,
which makes our interactions so much better.

KICKSTANDS
One dysfunctional behavior common in many families is using
one member as what I call a *kickstand*. Whenever two family
members have a problem with each other, one or both will bring
in a third member, and respond to anxiety between each other by
shifting the focus onto this third member. Two are on the inside
and one is on the outside. For example, rather than mom con-
fronting dad about her frustration with him, she might vent on
her son. In doing so, she will pass the anxiety onto her son. This
process allows space for character assassination. Mom will be
speaking from years of hurt and anger. It also puts the son in an
unfair position. This creates cracks in the family container.

Don't be a kickstand.

If all family members refuse to be kickstands, the person with
the conflict will be forced to resolve their issues on their own. If
you refuse to engage in the triangle by telling them how you feel
and why (you can explain this kickstand concept and the consequences), they will be forced to express themselves to the person
with whom they have a conflict on their own. This means that
they will be forced to exercise their Transparency muscles and
create their Stance. By not being a kickstand, you are giving them
tools to build their own safe container as well as a safe container
for the family.

Sometimes, however, family members decide to hold emotions inside and be angry at you, and that's the hard part, because
you're going to feel guilty. You're going to want to make everything

okay. You're going to feel like you're being a bad daughter, sister, mother—whatever relationship you have with that family member. But that's just the pain of growing, and you should never sacrifice your own growth for someone else. You must set the example. Whether they learn from it or not is on them and you can't do anything about that. That doesn't mean that you don't love them; it simply means that you're doing everything you believe is healthy and best for the family, with yourself included in that mix.

> See, I think there are roads that lead us to each other. But in my family, there were no roads—just underground tunnels. I think we all got lost in those underground tunnels. No, not lost. We just lived there. [9]
> —Benjamin Alire Saenz

If you live your truth around your family—if you live in your Solid Self and refuse to be a kickstand—the family dynamic will change. It may take years, but it will eventually change, because you are an important part of the family dynamic. This is not psychology; it's physics. For every action, there's a reaction. Most likely, the reaction of your family will come in the form of resistance: You are tipping the boat, and they are afraid to fall into the water. Don't mistake that for them not loving you—or what you're doing for a sign that you don't love them. Be patient. Remember, your focus is not to change them; it's just to live the truest version of you. How do you do that? By taking to heart what I discuss in this book: By building yourself a brand new container and protecting yourself and your growth, you will shift your family dynamic. This creates a space for change. Your difference will break the pattern of behavior, and hopefully your change will ignite change in others. This is the same concept that is used in a Therapeutic Community.

Living in your Solid Self around your family might be the most difficult piece in building your new container. It requires a tremendous amount of courage and strength because you're shaking a foundation: You're cracking concrete that's been set down since childhood. The amount of work you do in Transparency and Stance will determine whether you use a jackhammer or a toothpick.

IN A SHOT GLASS
To create your container, you must:

- Continue to practice Transparency and have a Stance.

- Create a structure (a program based around your Self-Care Practice).

- Create your Top Five (friends that will make you the best version of you. Use your strainer).

- Stay Solid around your family (be transparent, hold on to your Stance, and don't be a kickstand).

Chapter Five

Maintaining Your Safe Container

Small hairline cracks can form in our containers. We don't always notice them, because they happen gradually, sinking us back into our quicksand. Here are six areas to explore and repair.

- Thought patterns
- Significance
- Micro- vs. Macro-living
- Reducing your noise
- Shifting perspective
- Your center of gravity

THOUGHT PATTERNS

Life is all about how you think, and your feelings are right behind your thoughts. If your thinking is unhealthy, how you feel about yourself will most likely hold you down. Feelings can overpower you and send you into a very deep ditch.

Situations aren't what make us feel and react the way we do; it's how we *perceive* those situations. Our thoughts and beliefs about events influence our emotions and actions. And our perception is created from our story.

> We don't see things as they are, we see them as we are.
> —Anaïs Nin

Most of us are so focused on getting somewhere or obtaining something that we forget that happiness lives in the way we see the world, our beliefs about ourselves, and the way we think. What you think and *how* you think will determine your path.

> The primary cause of unhappiness is never the situation, but your thoughts about it. Be aware of the thoughts you are thinking.
> —Eckhart Tolle

COGNITIVE DISTORTIONS: THE BASICS

Talking about how you think leads us to the concept of cognitive distortions, which are simply the ways our mind convinces us of something that isn't really true. These inaccurate thoughts are usually used to reinforce negative thinking or emotions—telling ourselves things that sound rational and accurate, but that really only keep us feeling bad about ourselves by playing broken records.

There are many types of cognitive distortions, but here are what I believe are the nine most common ones. See if any resonate with you.

1. FILTERING

This happens when we take negative details and magnify them, while filtering out all positive aspects of a situation. For instance, a person may pick out a single, unpleasant detail and dwell on it exclusively so that their vision of reality becomes darkened or distorted. This happened a lot to me when I was screenwriting: After I spent four months working on a screenplay and finished a first draft, I would give it to my friends for some honest feedback. Even if everyone liked it except for one person, I would think the script was shit. I would focus on the one negative opinion instead of all the other positive ones. This thinking translated into the notes as well: Instead of appreciating all the positive notes, I would only focus on the negative notes. This type of thinking made it nearly impossible to see my gifts. Instead I only saw my faults—and if that's all I see, eventually my beliefs about myself and my behavior will match that.

> Some people grumble that roses have thorns; I am grateful that thorns have roses.
> —Alphonse Karr

Famous people filter as well. David Sedaris once wrote an essay about how, when he speaks to a packed auditorium filled with hundreds of adoring fans, he will notice the one person who gets up and leaves the row. He'll then obsess over why that person left, to the point where that one person will define how he perceives his entire performance—he'll think of it as shitty, even though there might be 800 people who sat there enthralled by his talk—even though, in reality, that person might have left to go to the restroom, not because he didn't like what Sedaris was saying. Johnny Depp claims he never watches anything he does. Many actors feel similarly—it can be hard for them to watch themselves, because they often pick out one bad scene to focus on (out of the hundreds of other good scenes). Usually when people are praised for their successes and achievement, they start to only focus on their failures and shortcomings.

Do you filter? If so, when? Write it down. How does that type of thinking bring you anxiety? What type of behaviors are a result of this distortion? How does it play out in your day-to-day life?

2. POLARIZED THINKING (OR
BLACK AND WHITE THINKING)

When we engage in polarized thinking, things are either black or white. We have to be perfect or we're a failure; there is no middle ground. You place people or situations in "either/or" categories, with no shades of gray and no room for the complexity inherent in most people and situations. If your performance falls short of perfect, you see yourself as a total failure. Many athletes struggle with this: There is no second place—you either win or you lose; all or nothing. This mindset can set you up for a huge fall. If you don't succeed, you fail. That's a lot of pressure and it usually strips away the enjoyment of the activity and keeps you in your head, which, in turn, always affects your performance in a negative way.

Imagine when this type of thinking translates into areas of your life where you don't have a lot of control. In relationships, for example, you are only one half of the equation. Even if you are "perfect," you'll always only be fifty percent of the relationship. If you think in black and white, any disagreement or argument can make you question everything. Again, with this type of thinking everything is at stake, which means that you will always live under a cloud of free-floating anxiety.

Is your thinking polarized? If so, when? In what areas of your life is it the strongest? What type of behaviors are a result of this distortion? How does it play out in your day-to-day life?

3. OVERGENERALIZATION

In this cognitive distortion, we come to a general conclusion based on a single incident or a single piece of evidence. If something bad happens once, we then expect it to happen over and over again. A person may see a single unpleasant event as part of a never-ending pattern of defeat. This happens a lot when we're dating: *She didn't return my text in three seconds, so she must be dating someone else now.* Or you try to switch things up and make love to your wife in the middle of the night and she doesn't feel like it, so you perceive that as her not being as attracted to you as she used to. Or if you're a new athlete and you score toward the bottom on your first competition, you believe that this will be the case in every competition.

Do you overgeneralize? If so, when? How does that type of thinking create anxiety? What types of behaviors are a result of this distortion? How does it play out in your day-to-day life?

4. JUMPING TO CONCLUSIONS

This is a very common one—we have all done it at one time or another. We often think we know what people are feeling and why they act the way they do. In particular, we think we are able to determine how people are feeling toward us. For example, you may conclude that someone is reacting negatively toward you, but you don't actually bother to find out if you are correct. You make an assumption, and now you've distanced yourself from that person. Later, you find out that it had nothing to do with you; maybe your friend's father passed away or they are in the process of getting a divorce.

Another way to jump to a conclusion is by anticipating that things will turn out badly, and feeling convinced that your prediction is already an established fact. You have a raise coming up, but you believe you won't get it because you haven't been getting along with your boss. Or you start a blog and don't get the following you expected in the first month, so you believe that you can't write.

Do you jump to conclusions? If so, when? How does that type of thinking create anxiety? What types of behaviors are a result of this distortion? How does it play out in your day-to-day life?

5. CATASTROPHIZING

I call this living in *what-ifs*. We expect disaster to strike, no matter what. This is also referred to as "magnifying or minimizing." We hear about a problem and use *what if* questions (e.g., *What if tragedy strikes? What if it happens to me? What if I starve? What if I die?*). In a nutshell, we sabotage any possibility of anything good happening before we even try. Usually this is all about fear and control, or being afraid and not having control of outcomes. This type of thinking creates a wall and prevents you from accomplishing your goals. It becomes an excuse to not pursue anything. *What if the plane goes down? What if my idea doesn't work? What if no one likes it? What if I can't find a job? What if she doesn't like me? What if I can't get it up? What if he doesn't understand? What if I never get married?*

I always ask my clients to play out their *what-ifs*. Usually it's never as bad or tragic as they imagine it in their heads. The sky didn't fall. No one died. And after they get past that, they start coming up with solutions to their *what-ifs*. Now they are in a growth mindset instead of a fixed one.

Do you catastrophize? If so, when? How does that type of thinking create anxiety? What behavior is a result of this distortion? How does it play out in your day-to-day life?

6. PERSONALIZATION

Personalization happens when we believe that everything others do or say is some kind of direct, personal reaction to us. We all know this kind of person, right? We call them "too sensitive." But what if this were actually a cognitive thing instead of a sensitivity thing?

Our ego causes us to bring everything back to us: We believe people act a certain way because of something we did or said when it may have nothing to do with us. We personalize things because we are insecure about ourselves, unsure, and/or afraid to express ourselves and communicate what we feel.

There's a common saying: *What someone thinks about you is none of your business.* It's nearly impossible to be your Solid Self if you live with this cognitive distortion. This type of thinking compels us to seek validation and approval, and when you seek, you can't give your true self.

People who engage in personalization may also see themselves as the cause of an unhealthy external event for which they actually were not responsible.

For example: *We were late to the dinner party and caused the hostess to overcook the meal. If I had only pushed my husband to leave on time, this wouldn't have happened. Or: If I had more sex with my boyfriend and gave him what he wanted sexually, he wouldn't have cheated on me. Or: I know I wasn't driving, but if I didn't take so long to get ready, we wouldn't have gotten into the car accident.*

Do you personalize? If so, when? How does that type of thinking create anxiety? What behavior is a result of this distortion? How does it play out in your day-to-day life?

NOTES

1. Jason Silva, "Jason Silva Shares His Best Advice." (YouTube video, 02:13. Posted April 2012). https://www.youtube.com/watch?v=UWvJ9IjdHxM.

2. Steve Maraboli, *Unapologetically You: Reflections on Life and the Human Experience*. (Port Washington, NY: Better Today, 2013).

3. Brené Brown, "The Power of Vulnerability." (Speech, TEDxHouston, Houston, June 2010).

4. Ray Bradbury, *Fahrenheit 451*. (New York: Simon and Schuster, 1967).

5. Eckhart Tolle, *The Power of Now: A Guide to Spiritual Enlightenment*. (Novato, CA: New World Library, 1999).

6. Melody Beattie, *The Language of Letting Go*. (Center City, MN: Hazelden, 1990).

7. John Mordechai Gottman and Joan DeClaire, *Raising an Emotionally Intelligent Child*. (New York, NY: Simon & Schuster, 1998).

8. Thich Nhat Hanh, *The Miracle of Mindfulness* (Copyright © 1975, 1976 by Thich Nhat Hanh. Preface and English translation Copyright © 1975, 1976, 1987 by Mobi Ho. Reprinted by permission of Beacon Press, Boston).

9. Benjamin Alire Sáenz, *Last Night I Sang to the Monster*. (El Paso, TX: Cinco Puntos Press, 2009).

ABOUT THE AUTHOR

John Kim is a licensed Marriage Family Therapist. In 2010, he started a blog partly to document his own journey and partly to create a dialogue to help others. Coaching people online was not his intention, but here's what happened: By the end of that year he had two clients; by the end of the second year, he had coached over 100 people from all over the globe, including individuals, couples, and groups. All of this was from his computer. Because of the overwhelming response to this online community, John quit his 9 to 5 job and opened a "public" practice. He defines his practice as "public" because he does everything online, from individual and couple sessions to group work.

Today, The Angry Therapist is not just a blog/practice; it's a Therapeutic Community where people can rebuild themselves through others.

Meet The Angry Therapist at theangrytherapist.com and rebuild your container with others at shft.us.

You can also find The Angry Therapist on social media:
Facebook: www.facebook.com/theangrytherapist
Instagram: @theangrytherapist

RELATED TITLES

Bent, Anne Clendening

Fear, Illustrated, Julie M. Elman

The Idealist's Survival Kit, Alessandra Pigni

In Real Life, Jon Mitchell

Happiness, Thich Nhat Hanh

The Mindful Athlete, George Mumford

Ten Breaths to Happiness, Glen Schneider

**PARALLAX
PRESS**

Parallax Press is a nonprofit publisher, founded and inspired by Zen Master Thich Nhat Hanh. We publish books on mindfulness in daily life and are committed to making these teachings accessible to everyone and preserving them for future generations. We do this work to alleviate suffering and contribute to a more just and joyful world.

For a copy of the catalog, please contact:

Parallax Press
P.O. Box 7355
Berkeley, CA 94707
parallax.org